IN THE
YULE-LOG GLOW

Book IV

Various Authors

CHRISTMAS POEMS FROM
'ROUND THE WORLD

"Sic as folk tell ower at a winter ingle"

Scott

Editor: **Harrison S. Morris**

[ZHINGOORA BOOKS]

This edition is published by
Zhingoora Books.

The Cover is Designed by Pallav Sethiya.

CONTENTS OF BOOK IV.

A Happy New Year

New-Year's Gifts

The End of the Play

Finis

FOOTNOTES:

[A] By the courtesy of Messrs. Houghton, Mifflin & Co.

[B] By the courtesy of Messrs. Charles Scribners' Sons.

[C] By the courtesy of Messrs. Harper & Bros.

Sung Under The Window.

"This carol they began that hourWith a hey, and a ho, and a hey nonino!"

Shakespeare.

WHO'S THERE?

Nowell, nowell, nowell, nowell,Who ys there that syngith so, nowell, nowell, nowell?

I am here, syre Christmasse!Well come, my lord syre Christmasse,Welcome to us all, bothe more and lesse,Come nere, nowell!

Dieu vous garde, beau syre, tydinges you bryng:A mayd hath born a chylde full yong,The weche causeth yew for to syng,Nowell!

Criste is now born of a pure mayde,In an oxe stalle he ys layde,Wher'for syng we alle atte abraydeNowell!

Bebbex bien par tutte la company,Make gode chere and be right mery,And syng with us now joyfully,Nowell!

GOD REST YOU MERRY, GENTLEMEN.

God rest you merry, gentlemen,Let nothing you dismay,For Jesus Christ our SaviourWas born upon this dayTo save us all from Satan's powerWhen we were gone astray.O tidings of comfort and joy,For Jesus Christ our Saviour was born on Christmas day.

In Bethlehem in JewryThis blessed babe was born,And laid within a mangerUpon this blessed morn;The which His mother MaryNothing did take in scorn.O tidings, etc.

From God our Heavenly FatherA blessed angel came,And unto certain shepherdsBrought tidings of the same,How that in Bethlehem was bornThe Son of God by name.O tidings, etc.

Fear not, then said the angel,Let nothing you affright,This day is born a SaviourOf virtue, power, and might;So frequently to vanquish allThe friends of Satan quite.O tidings, etc.

The shepherds at those tidingsRejoicéd much in mind,And left their flocks a-feedingIn tempest, storm, and wind,And went to Bethlehem straightwayThis blessed babe to find.O tidings, etc.

But when to Bethlehem they came,Whereat this infant lay,They found Him in a mangerWhere oxen feed on hay;His mother Mary kneelingUnto the Lord did pray.O tidings, etc.

Now to the Lord sing praises,All you within this place,And with true love and brotherhoodEach other now embrace;This holy tide of ChristmasAll others doth deface.O tidings, etc.

WELCOME YULE.

Welcome Yule, thou merry man, In worship of this holy day.

Welcome be thou, heaven-king, Welcome born in one morning, Welcome for whom we shall sing, Welcome Yule.

Welcome be ye, Stephen and John, Welcome Innocents, every one, Welcome Thomas Martyr one, Welcome Yule.

Welcome be ye, good New Year, Welcome Twelfth Day, both in fere, [D] Welcome saintés lef[E] and dear, Welcome Yule.

Welcome be ye, Candlemas, Welcome be ye, Queen of Bliss, Welcome both to more and less, Welcome Yule.

Welcome be ye that are here, Welcome all and make good cheer; Welcome all, another year, Welcome Yule.

Ritson's Ancient Songs.

FOOTNOTES:

[D] Together.

[E] Loved.

ANGEL HERALDS.

As Joseph was a-walking,He heard an angel sing:"This night shall be bornOur Heavenly King;

"He neither shall be bornIn housen nor in hall,Nor in the place of Paradise,But in an ox's stall;

"He neither shall be clothédIn purple nor in pall,But all in fair linen,As we were babies all.

"He neither shall be rockedIn silver nor in gold,But in a wooden cradleThat rocks on the mould.

"He neither shall be christenedIn white wine nor in red,But with fair spring-waterWith which we were christenéd."

THE MATCHLESS MAIDEN.

I sing of a maidenThat is makeless;[F]King of all kingsTo her son she ches;[G]

He came also[H] stillThere His mother was,As dew in AprilThat falleth on the grass.

He came also stillTo His mother's bower,As dew in AprilThat falleth on the flower.

He came also stillThere His mother lay,As dew in AprilThat falleth on the spray.

Mother and maidenWas never none but she;Well may such a ladyGod's mother be.

Wright's Songs and Carols.

FOOTNOTES:

[F]Matchless.

[G]Chose.

[H]As.

REMEMBER, O THOU MAN.

Remember, O thou Man, O thou Man, O thou Man; Remember, O thou Man, Thy time is spent. Remember, O thou Man, How thou earnest to me then, And I did what I can, Therefore repent.

Remember Adam's fall, O thou Man, O thou Man; Remember Adam's fall From Heaven to Hell. Remember Adam's fall, How we were condemnéd all To Hell perpetual, There for to dwell.

Remember God's goodness, O thou Man, O thou Man; Remember God's goodness And promise made. Remember God's goodness, How His only Son He sent Our sins for to redress, Be not afraid.

The Angels all did sing, O thou Man, O thou Man; The Angels all did sing On Sion hill. The Angels all did sing Praises to our heavenly king, And peace to man living, With right good-will.

The Shepherds amazed was, O thou Man, O thou Man; The Shepherds amazed was To hear the angels sing. The Shepherds amazed was How this should come to pass, That Christ our Messias Should be our King.

To Bethlehem did they go, O thou Man, O thou Man; To Bethlehem did they go This thing to see. To Bethlehem did they go To see whether it was so, Whether Christ was born or no, To set us free.

As the Angels before did say, O thou Man, O thou Man; As the Angels before did say, So it came to pass. As the Angels before did say, They found Him wrapt in hay In a manger where He lay, So poor He was.

In Bethlehem was He born,O thou Man, O thou Man;In Bethlehem was He bornFor mankind dear.In Bethlehem was He bornFor us that were forlorn,And therefore took no scornOur sins to bear.

In a manger laid He was,O thou Man, O thou Man;In a manger laid He wasAt this time present.In a manger laid He wasBetween an ox and an ass,And all for our trespass,Therefore repent.

Give thanks to God always,O thou Man, O thou Man;Give thanks to God alwaysWith hearts most jolly.Give thanks to God alwaysupon this blessed day,Let all men sing and say,Holy, Holy.

Ravenscroft's Melismata, a.d. 1611.

THE SINGERS IN THE SNOW.

God bless the master of this houseAnd all that are therein,And to begin this Christmas tideWith mirth now let us sing.For the Saviour of all peopleUpon this time was born,Who did from death deliver us.When we were left forlorn.

Then let us all most merry be,And sing with cheerful voice,For we have good occasion nowThis time for to rejoice.For, etc.

Then put away contention all,And fall no more at strife,Let every man with cheerfulnessEmbrace his loving wife.For, etc.

With plenteous food your houses store,Provide some wholesome cheer,And call your friends togetherThat live both far and near.For, etc.

Then let us all most merry be,Since that we are come here,And we do hope before we partTo taste some of your beer.For, etc.

Your beer, your beer, your Christmas beer,That seems to be so strong;And we do wish that Christmas-tideWas twenty times so long.For, etc.

Then sing with voices cheerfully,For Christ this time was born,Who did from death deliver us,When we were left forlorn.For, etc.

A CHRISTMAS CHORUS.

Here is joy for every age— Every generation;Prince and peasant, chief and sage,Every tongue and nation,Every tongue and nation,Every rank and station,Hath to-day salvation.Alleluia!

When the world drew near its close,Came our Lord and leader;From the lily came the rose,From the bush the cedar,From the bush the cedar,From the judge the pleader,From the saint the feeder.Alleluia!

God, that came on earth this morn,In a manger lying,Hallow'd birth by being born,Vanquished death by dying,Vanquished death by dying,Rallied back the flying,Ended sin and sighing.Alleluia!

THREE SHIPS.

I saw three ships come sailing in, On Christmas day, on Christmas day; I saw three ships come sailing in, On Christmas day in the morning.

And what was in those ships all three, On Christmas day, on Christmas day? And what was in those ships all three, On Christmas day in the morning?

Our Saviour Christ and His lady, On Christmas day, on Christmas day; Our Saviour Christ and His lady, On Christmas day in the morning.

Pray whither sailed those ships all three, On Christmas day, on Christmas day? Pray whither sailed those ships all three, On Christmas day in the morning?

O they sailed into Bethlehem, On Christmas day, on Christmas day, O they sailed into Bethlehem, On Christmas day in the morning.

And all the bells on earth shall ring, On Christmas day, on Christmas day; And all the bells on earth shall ring, On Christmas day in the morning.

And all the angels in heaven shall sing, On Christmas day, on Christmas day; And all the angels in heaven shall sing, On Christmas day in the morning.

And all the souls on earth shall sing,On Christmas day, on Christmas day;And all the souls on earth shall sing,On Christmas day in the morning.

Then let us all rejoice amain,On Christmas day, on Christmas day;Then let us all rejoice amain,On Christmas day in the morning.

JACOB'S LADDER.

As Jacob with travel was weary one day,At night on a stone for a pillow he lay;He saw in a vision a ladder so highThat its foot was on earth and its top in the sky.Hallelujah to Jesus, who died on the tree,And hath rais'd up a ladder of mercy for me.

This ladder is high, it is strong and well made,Hath stood hundreds of years and is not yet decayed;Many millions have climbed it and reached Zion's hill,And thousands, by faith, are climbing it still.Hallelujah, etc.

Come, let us ascend, all may climb it who will,For the angels of Jacob are guarding it still;And remember each step that by faith we pass o'er,Some prophet or martyr hath trod it before.Hallelujah, etc.

And when we arrive at the haven of rest,We shall hear the glad word: Come up hither, ye blest!Here are regions of light, here are mansions of bliss,Oh, who would not climb such a ladder as this?Hallelujah, etc.

SAINT STEPHEN, THE CLERK.

Saint Stephen was a clerkIn King Herod's hall,And servéd him of bread and clothAs ever king befall.

Stephen out of kitchen cameWith boar's head on hand,He saw a star was fair and brightOver Bethlehem stand.

He kist adown the boar's headAnd went into the hall:"I forsake thee, King Herod,And thy workés all.

"I forsake thee, King Herod,And thy workés all;There is a child in Bethlehem bornIs better than we all."

"What aileth thee, Stephen?What is thee befall?Lacketh thee either meat or drinkIn King Herod's hall?"

"Lacketh me neither meat ne drinkIn King Herod's hall;There is a child in Bethlehem bornIs better than we all."

"What aileth thee, Stephen?Art thou wode,[I] or thou ginnest to breed?[J]Lacketh thee either gold or fee,Or any rich weed?"[K]

"Lacketh me neither gold nor fee,Ne none rich weed;There is a child in Bethlehem bornShall helpen us at our need."

"That is also sooth,[L] Stephen,Also sooth i-wisAs this capon crowé shallThat lieth here in my dish."

That word was not so soon said,That word in that hall,The capon crew *Christus natus est*Among the lordés all.

"Riseth up, my tormentors,By two and all by oneAnd leadeth Stephen out of this town,And stoneth him with stone."

Tooken they StephenAnd stoned him in the way,And therefore is his evenOn Christés own day.

FOOTNOTES:

[I]Mad.

[J]Scold.

[K]Dress.

[L]As true.

THE CARNAL AND THE CRANE.

As I pass'd by a riverside,And there as I did reign,[M]In argument I chanced to hearA Carnal[N] and a Crane.

The Carnal said unto the Crane,If all the world should turn,Before we had the Father,But now we have the Son!

From whence does the Son come?From where and from what place?He said, In a manger,Between an ox and ass!

I pray thee, said the Carnal,Tell me before thou go,Was not the mother of JesusConceived by the Holy Ghost?

She was the purest Virgin,And the cleanest from sin;She was the handmaid of our Lord,And mother of our King.

Where is the golden cradleThat Christ was rockèd in?Where are the silken sheetsThat Jesus was wrapt in?

A manger was the cradleThat Christ was rockèd in;The provender the asses leftSo sweetly He slept on.

There was a star in the West-land,So bright did it appearInto King Herod's chamber,And where King Herod were.

The Wise Men soon espied it,And told the king on high,A princely babe was born that nightNo king could e'er destroy.

If this be true, King Herod said,As thou tellest unto me,This roasted cock that lies in the dishShall crow full fences[O] three.

The cock soon freshly feathered wasBy the work of God's own hand,And then three fences crowéd heIn the dish where he did stand.

Rise up, rise up, you merry men all,See that you ready be,All children under two years oldNow slain they all shall be.

Then Jesus, ah! and Joseph,And Mary that was so pure,They travelled into Egypt,As you shall find it sure.

And when they came to Egypt's land,Amongst those fierce wild beasts,Mary, she being weary,Must needs sit down to rest.

Come sit thee down, says Jesus,Come sit thee down by me,And thou shalt see how these wild beastsDo come and worship me.

First came the lovely lion,Which Jesu's grace did spring,And of the wild beasts in the field,The lion shall be the king.

We'll choose our virtuous princes,Of birth and high degree,In every sundry nation,Where'er we come and see.

Then Jesus, ah! and Joseph,And Mary, that was unknown,They travelled by a husbandman,Just while his seed was sown.

God speed thee, man! said Jesus,Go fetch thy ox and wain,And carry home thy corn againWhich thou this day hast sown.

The husbandman fell on his knees,Even before his face;Long time hast Thou been looked for,But now Thou art come at last.

And I myself do now believeThy name is Jesus called;Redeemer of mankind Thou art,Though undeserving all.

The truth, man, thou hast spoken,Of it thou may'st be sure,For I must lose my precious bloodFor thee and thousands more.

If any one should come this way,And inquire for me alone,Tell them that Jesus passed by,As thou thy seed did sow.

After that there came King Herod,With his train so furiously,Inquiring of the husbandman,Whether Jesus passed by.

Why, the truth it must be spoke,And the truth it must be known,For Jesus passéd by this wayWhen my seed was sown.

But now I have it reapen,And some laid on my wain,Ready to fetch and carryInto my barn again.

Turn back, says the captain,Your labor and mine's in vain,It's full three-quarters of a yearSince he his seed sown.

So Herod was deceivédBy the work of God's own hand,And further he proceededInto the Holy Land.

There's thousands of children young,Which for His sake did die;Do not forbid those little ones,And do not them deny.

The truth now I have spoken,And the truth now I have shown,Even the blessed Virgin,She's now brought forth a Son.

FOOTNOTES:

[M]Run.

[N] Crow.

[O] Rounds.

THE HOLY WELL.

As it fell out one May morning,And upon one bright holiday,Sweet Jesus asked of His dear mother,If He might go to play.

To play, to play, sweet Jesus shall go,And to play pray get you gone;And let me hear of no complaintAt night when you come home.

Sweet Jesus went down to yonder townAs far as the Holy Well,And there did see as fine childrenAs any tongue can tell.

He said, God bless you every one,And your bodies Christ save and see:Little children, shall I play with you,And you shall play with me?

But they made answer to Him, No:They were lords' and ladies' sons;And He, the meanest of them all,Was but a maiden's child, born in an ox's stall.

Sweet Jesus turned Him around,And He neither laughed nor smiled,But the tears came trickling from His eyesLike water from the skies.

Sweet Jesus turned Him about,To His mother's dear home went He,And said, I have been in yonder town,As far as you can see.

I have been down in yonder townAs far as the Holy Well,There did I meet as fine childrenAs any tongue can tell.

I bid God bless them every one, And their bodies Christ save and see: Little children, shall I play with you, And you shall play with me?

But they made answer to me, No: They were lords' and ladies' sons; And I, the meanest of them all, Was but a maiden's child, born in an ox's stall.

Though you are but a maiden's child, Born in an ox's stall, Thou art the Christ, the King of heaven, And the Saviour of them all.

Sweet Jesus, go down to yonder town As far as the Holy Well, And take away those sinful souls, And dip them deep in hell.

Nay, nay, sweet Jesus said, Nay, nay, that may not be; For there are too many sinful souls Crying out for the help of me.

THE HOLLY AND THE IVY.

The Holly and the Ivy,Now both are full well grown;Of all the trees that spring in wood,The holly bears the crown.The holly bears a blossomAs white as a lily flow'r;And Mary bore sweet Jesus ChristTo be our sweet Saviour.

The holly bears a berryAs red as any blood,And Mary bore sweet Jesus ChristTo do poor sinners good.The holly bears a prickleAs sharp as any thorn,And Mary bore sweet Jesus ChristOn Christmas Day in the morn.

The holly bears a barkAs bitter as any gall,And Mary bore sweet Jesus ChristFor to redeem us all.The holly and the ivyNow are both well grown;Of all the trees that are in the wood,The holly bears the crown.

THE CONTEST OF THE VINES.

Nay, ivy, nay, It shall not be, I wis; Let holly have the mastery, As the manner is.

Holly stand in the hall, Fair to behold; Ivy stand without the door, She is full sore a-cold. Nay, ivy, nay, etc.

Holly and his merry men They dancen and they sing; Ivy and her maidens They weepen and they wring. Nay, ivy, nay, etc.

Ivy hath a kybe, [P] She caught it with the cold; So mot they all have ae, [Q] That with ivy hold. Nay, ivy, nay, etc.

Holly hath berries As red as any rose, The forester and the hunters Keep them from the does. Nay, ivy, nay, etc.

Ivy hath berries As black as any sloe; There come the owl And eat him as she go. Nay, ivy, nay, etc.

Holly hath birdés A full fair flock, The nightingale, the popinjay, The gentle laverock. Nay, ivy, nay, etc.

Good ivy, What birdés hast thou? None but the howlet That krey [R] "How, how."

Nay, ivy, nay, It shall not be, I wis; Let holly have the mastery, As the manner is.

33

FOOTNOTES:

[P] Chapped skin.

[Q] So may all have.

[R] Cries.

ANE SANG OF THE BIRTH OF CHRIST.

A SCOTCH CAROL.

I come from hevin to tellThe best nowellis that ever befell;To you this tythinges trew I bring,And I will of them say and sing:

This day to yow is borne ane childeOf Marie meike and Virgine mylde,That blessit barne, bining and kynde,Sall yow rejoyce baith heart and mynd.

My saull and lyfe, stand up and seeQuha lyes in ane cribe of tree,Quhat babe is that, so gude and faire?It is Christ, God's sonne and aire.

O God, that made all creature,How art Thow becum so pure,That on the hay and stray will lyeAmang the asses, oxin, and kye!

O my deir hert, young Jesus sweit,Prepare Thy creddill in my spreit,And I sall rocke Thee in my hert,And never mair from Thee depart.

But I sall praise Thee evermoirWith sangs sweit unto Thy gloir,The knees of my hert sall I bow,And sing that right Balululow.

CHRISTMAS MINSTRELSY.

The minstrels played their Christmas tuneTo-night beneath my cottage eaves;While smitten by a lofty moon,The encircling laurels thick with leaves,Gave back a rich and dazzling sheen,That overpowered their natural green.

Through hill and valley every breezeHad sunk to rest with folded wings:Keen was the air, but could not freezeNor check the music of the strings;So stout and hardy were the bandThat scraped the chords with strenuous hand.

And who but listened?—till was paidRespect to every inmate's claim,The greeting given, the music playedIn honor of each household name,Duly pronounced with lusty call,And a merry Christmas wished to all.

O Brother! I revere the choiceThat took thee from thy native hills;And it is given thee to rejoice:Though public care full often tills(Heaven only witness of the toil)A barren and ungrateful soil.

Yet would that thou, with me and mine,Hadst heard this never-failing rite;And seen on other faces shineA true revival of the lightWhich nature, and these rustic powers,In simple childhood, spread through ours!

For pleasure hath not ceased to waitOn these expected annual rounds,Whether the rich man's sumptuous gateCall forth the unelaborate sounds,Or they are offered at the doorThat guard the lowliest of the poor.

How touching, when at midnight sweepSnow-muffled winds, and all is dark,To hear—and sink again in sleep!Or at an earlier call, to mark,By blazing fire, the still suspenseOf self-complacent innocence;

The mutual nod—the grave disguiseOf hearts with gladness brimming o'er,And some unhidden tears that riseFor names once heard, and heard no more;Tears brightened by the serenadeFor infant in the cradle laid!

Ah! not for emerald fields alone,With ambient streams more pure and brightThan fabled Cytherea's zoneGlittering before the Thunderer's sight,Is to my heart of hearts endeared,The ground where we were born and reared!

Hail, ancient manners! sure defence,Where they survive, of wholesome laws:Remnants of love whose modest senseThus into narrow room withdraws;Hail, usages of pristine mould,And ye that guard them, Mountains old!

Bear with me, Brother! quench the thoughtThat slights this passion or condemns;If thee fond fancy ever broughtFrom the proud margin of the Thames,And Lambeth's venerable towers,To humble streams and greener bowers.

Yes, they can make, who fail to findShort leisure even in busiest days,Moments to cast a look behind,And profit by those kindly raysThat through the clouds do sometimes steal,And all the far-off past reveal.

Hence, while the imperial city's dinBeats frequent on thy satiate ear,A pleased attention I may winTo agitations less severe,That neither overwhelm nor cloy,But fill the hollow vale with joy!

William Wordsworth.

THE OLD, OLD STORY.

Listen, Lordings, unto me, a tale I will you tell,Which, as on this night of glee, in David's town befell.Joseph came from Nazareth, with Mary that sweet maid;Weary were they, nigh to death; and for a lodging pray'd.Sing high, sing high, sing low, sing low,Sing high, sing low, sing to and fro,Go tell it out with speed,Cry out and shout all round about,That Christ is born indeed.

In the inn they found no room; a scanty bed they made:Soon a Babe from Mary's womb was in the manger laid.Forth He came as light through glass: He came to save us all,In the stable ox and ass before their Maker fall.Sing high, sing low, etc.

Shepherds lay afield that night, to keep the silly sheep,Hosts of angels in their sight came down from heaven's high steep.Tidings! tidings! unto you: to you a Child is born,Purer than the drops of dew, and brighter than the morn.Sing high, sing low, etc.

Onward then the angels sped, the shepherds onward went,God was in His manger bed, in worship low they bent.In the morning see ye mind, my masters one and all,At the altar Him to find who lay within the stall.Sing high, sing low, etc.

H. R. Bramley.

A CHRISTMAS BALLAD.

Outlanders, whence come ye last? *The snow in the street and the wind on the door.* Through what green sea and great have ye past? *Minstrels and maids, stand forth on the floor.*

From far away, O masters mine, *The snow in the street and the wind on the door.* We come to bear you goodly wine: *Minstrels and maids, stand forth on the floor.*

From far away we come to you, *The snow in the street and the wind on the door.* To tell of great tidings strange and true: *Minstrels and maids, stand forth on the floor.*

News, news of the Trinity, *The snow in the street and the wind on the door.* And Mary and Joseph from over the sea: *Minstrels and maids, stand forth on the floor.*

For as we wandered far and wide, *The snow in the street and the wind on the door.* What hope do ye deem there should us betide? *Minstrels and maids, stand forth on the floor.*

Under a bent when the night was deep, *The snow in the street and the wind on the door.* There lay three shepherds tending their sheep: *Minstrels and maids, stand forth on the floor.*

"O ye shepherds, what have ye seen, *The snow in the street and the wind on the door.* To slay your sorrow and heal your teen?" *Minstrels and maids, stand forth on the floor.*

"In an ox-stall this night we saw, *The snow in the street and the wind on the door.* A Babe and a maid without a flaw. *Minstrels and maids, stand forth on the floor.*

"There was an old man there beside, *The snow in the street and the wind, on the door.* His hair was white, and his hood was wide. *Minstrels and maids, stand forth on the floor.*

"And as we gazed this thing upon, *The snow in the street and the wind on the door.* Those twain knelt down to the Little One. *Minstrels and maids, stand forth on the floor.*

"And a marvellous song we straight did hear, *The snow in the street and the wind on the door.* That slew our sorrow and healed our care." *Minstrels and maids, stand forth on the floor.*

News of a fair and a marvellous thing, *The snow in the street and the wind on the door.* Nowell, nowell, nowell, we sing! *Minstrels and maids, stand forth on the floor.*

William Morris.

A FRENCH NOËL.

(TRANSLATED FROM GUI BARÔZAI.)

I hear along our streetPass the minstrel throngs;Hark! they play so sweet,On their hautboys, Christmas songs!Let us by the fireEver higherSing them till the night expire!

In December ringEvery day the chimes;Loud the gleemen singIn the streets their merry rhymes.Let us by the fire, etc.

Shepherds at the grange,Where the Babe was born,Sang, with many a change,Christmas carols until morn.Let us by the fire, etc.

These good people sangSongs devout and sweet;While the rafters rangThere they stood with freezing feet.Let us by the fire, etc.

Nuns in frigid cellsAt this holy tideFor want of something elseChristmas songs at times have tried.Let us by the fire, etc.

Washerwomen old,To the sound they beat,Sing by rivers coldWith uncovered heads and feet.Let us by the fire, etc.

Who by the fireside standsStamps his feet and sings;But he who blows his handsNot so gay a carol brings.Let us by the fire, etc.

Henry Wadsworth Longfellow.

MASTERS, IN THIS HALL.

"To Bethl'em did they go, the shepherds three;To Bethl'em did they go to see whe'r it were so or no,Whether Christ were born or noTo set men free."

Masters, in this hall,Hear ye news to-dayBrought over sea,And ever I you pray.*Nowell! Nowell! Nowell! Nowell!Sing we clear!Holpen are all folk on earth,Born is God's Son so dear.*

Going over the hills,Through the milk-white snow,Heard I ewes bleatWhile the winds did blow. *Nowell, etc.*

Shepherds many an oneSat among the sheep;No man spake more wordThan they had been asleep. *Nowell, etc.*

Quoth I, "Fellows mine,Why this guise sit ye?Making but dull cheer,Shepherds though ye be? *Nowell, etc.*

"Shepherds should of rightLeap, and dance, and sing;Thus to see you sitIs a right strange thing." *Nowell, etc.*

Quoth these fellows three,"To Bethl'em town we go,To see a Mighty LordLie in manger low." *Nowell, etc.*

"How name ye this Lord,Shepherds?" then said I."Very God," they said,"Come from Heaven high." *Nowell, etc.*

Then to Bethl'em townWe went two and two,And in a sorry placeHeard the oxen low. *Nowell, etc.*

Therein did we see A sweet and goodly May, And a fair old man; Upon the straw she lay. *Nowell, etc.*

And a little Child On her arm had she; "Wot ye who is this?" Said the hinds to me. *Nowell, etc.*

Ox and ass Him know, Kneeling on their knee: Wondrous joy had I This little Babe to see. *Nowell, etc.*

This is Christ the Lord: Masters, be ye glad! Christmas is come in, And no folk should be sad. *Nowell, etc.*

William Morris.

The Worship Of The Babe.

"Rejoice, our Saviour He was bornOn Christmas day in the morning."

Old Carol.

TO HIS SAVIOUR, A CHILD; A PRESENT, BY A CHILD.

Go, pretty child, and bear this flowerUnto thy little Saviour;And tell Him by that bud now blown,He is a Rose of Sharon known.When thou hast said so, stick it thereUpon His bib or stomacher;And tell Him, for good handsel too,That thou hast brought a whistle new,Made of a clean, strait oaten reedTo charm His cries at time of need.Tell Him for coral thou hast none,But if thou had'st He should have one;But poor thou art, and known to beEven as moneyless as He.Lastly, if thou can'st win a kissFrom those mellifluous lips of His,Then never take a second onTo spoil the first impression.

Robert Herrick.

HONOR TO THE KING.

Yet if his majesty our sovereign lordShould of his own accordFriendly himself invite,And say, "I'll be your guest tomorrow night,"How should we stir ourselves, call and commandAll hands to work: "Let no man idle stand.Set me fine Spanish tables in the hall,See they be fitted all;Let there be room to eat,And order taken that there want no meat.See every sconce and candlestick made bright,That without tapers they may give a light.Look to the presence; are the carpets spread,The dais o'er the head,The cushions in the chairs,And all the candles lighted on the stairs?Perfume the chambers, and in any caseLet each man give attendance in his place."Thus if the king were coming would we do,And 'twere good reason too;For 'tis a duteous thingTo show all honor to an earthly king,And after all our travail and our cost,So he be pleased, to think no labor lost.But at the coming of the King of Heaven,All's set at six and seven:We wallow in our sin,Christ cannot find a chamber in the inn.We entertain Him always like a stranger,And, as at first, still lodge Him in the manger.

Christ Church, Oxford, MS.

NEW PRINCE, NEW POMP.

Behold a silly, tender Babe,In freezing winter night,In homely manger trembling lies;Alas! a piteous sight.

The inns are full, no man will yieldThis little pilgrim bed;But forced He is with silly beastsIn crib to shroud His head.

Despise Him not for lying there,First what He is inquire;An orient pearl is often foundIn depth of dirty mire.

Weigh not His crib, His wooden dish,Nor beast that by Him feed;Weigh not His mother's poor attire,Nor Joseph's simple weed.

This stable is a prince's court,This crib His chair of state;The beasts are parcel of His pomp,The wooden dish His plate.

The persons in that poor attireHis royal liveries wear;The Prince himself is come from heaven,This pomp is praiséd there.

With joy approach, O Christian wight!Do homage to thy King;And highly praise this humble pompWhich He from heaven doth bring.

Robert Southwell.

OF THE EPIPHANY.

Fair eastern star, that art ordained to runBefore the sages, to the rising sun,Here cease thy course, and wonder that the cloudOf this poor stable can thy Maker shroud:Ye heavenly bodies glory to be bright,And are esteemed as ye are rich in light;But here on earth is taught a different way,Since under this low roof the Highest lay.Jerusalem erects her stately towers,Displays her windows and her bowers;Yet there thou must not cast a trembling spark,Let Herod's palace still continue dark;Each school and synagogue thy force repels,There pride enthroned in misty error dwells;The temple, where the priests maintain their quire,Shall taste no beam of thy celestial fire,While this weak cottage all thy splendor takes:A joyful gate of every chink it makes.Here shines no golden roof, no ivory stair,No king exalted in a stately chair,Girt with attendants, or by heralds styled,But straw and hay enwrap a speechless child.Yet Sabæ's lords before this babe unfoldTheir treasures, offering incense, myrrh, and gold.The crib becomes an altar; therefore diesNo ox nor sheep; for in their fodder liesThe Prince of Peace, who, thankful for His bed,Destroys those rites in which their blood was shed:The quintessence of earth He takes, and fees,And precious gums distilled from weeping trees;Rich metals and sweet odors now declareThe glorious blessings which His laws prepare,To clear us from the base and loathsome floodOf sense and make us fit for angel's food,Who lift to God for us the holy smokeOf fervent prayers with which we Him invoke,And try our actions in the searching fireBy which the seraphims our lips inspire:No muddy dross pure minerals shall infect,We shall exhale our vapors up direct:No storm shall cross, nor glittering lights defacePerpetual sighs which seek a happy place.

Sir John Beaumont.

A HYMN FOR THE EPIPHANY.

SUNG AS BY THE THREE KINGS.

1 King. Bright Babe! whose awful beauties make
The morn incur a sweet mistake;
2 King. For whom the officious heavens devise
To disinherit the sun's rise;
3 King. Delicately to displace
The day, and plant it fairer in Thy face;
1 King. O Thou born King of loves!
2 King. Of lights!
3 King. Of joys!

Chorus. Look up, sweet Babe, look up and see!
For love of Thee,
Thus far from home
The East is come
To seek herself in Thy sweet eyes.

1 King. We who strangely went astray,
Lost in a bright
Meridian night;
2 King. A darkness made of too much day;
3 King. Beckoned from far
By Thy fair star,
Lo, at last have found our way.

Chorus. To Thee, Thou Day of Night! Thou East of West!
Lo, we at last have found the way

To Thee, the world's great universal East,
The general and indifferent day.

1 King. All-circling point! all-centring sphere!
The world's one round eternal year:
2 King. Whose full and all-unwrinkled face
Nor sinks nor swells with time or place;
3 King. But everywhere and every while
Is one consistent solid smile,
1 King. Not vexed and tost,
2 King. 'Twixt spring and frost;
3 King. Nor by alternate shreds of light;
Sordidly shifting hands with shades and night.

Chorus. O little All, in Thy embrace,
The world lies warm and likes his place;
Nor does his full globe fail to be
Kissed on both his cheeks by Thee;
Time is too narrow for Thy year,
Nor makes the whole world Thy half-sphere.

Richard Crashaw.

A HYMN ON THE NATIVITY OF MY SAVIOUR.

I sing the birth was born to-night, The author both of life and light; The angels so did sound it. And like the ravished shepherds said, Who saw the light, and were afraid, Yet searched, and true they found it.

The Son of God th' eternal king, That did us all salvation bring, And freed the soul from danger; He whom the whole world could not take, The Word, which heaven and earth did make, Was now laid in a manger.

The Father's wisdom willed it so, The Son's obedience knew no No, Both wills were in one stature; And as that wisdom had decreed, The Word was now made flesh indeed, And took on Him our nature.

What comfort by Him do we win, Who made himself the price of sin, To make us heirs of glory! To see this babe all innocence; A martyr born in our defence; Can man forget the story?

Ben Jonson.

AT CHRISTMAS.

All after pleasures as I rid one day, My horse and I both tired, body and mind, With full cry of affections quite astray, I took up in the next inn I could find.

There, when I came, whom found I but my dear—My dearest Lord; expecting till the griefOf pleasures brought me to Him; ready thereTo be all passengers' most sweet relief?

O Thou, whose glorious, yet contracted light, Wrapt in night's mantle, stole into a manger;Since my dark soul and brutish is Thy right,To man, of all beasts, be not Thou a stranger;

Furnish and deck my soul, that Thou may'st haveA better lodging than a rock or grave.

The shepherds sing; and shall I silent be?My God, no hymn for Thee?My soul's a shepherd too; a flock it feedsOf thoughts and words and deeds;The pasture is Thy word, the stream Thy grace,Enriching every place.

Shepherd and flock shall sing, and all my powersOutsing the daylight hours.Then we will chide the sun for letting nightTake up his place and right:We sing one common Lord; wherefore He shouldHimself the candle hold.

I will go searching till I find a sunShall stay till we have done;A willing shiner, that shall shine as gladlyAs frost-nipt suns look sadly, Then we will sing and shine all our own day, And one another pay.

His beams shall cheer my breast; and both so twine, Till ev'n his beams sing and my music shine.

George Herbert.

NEW HEAVEN, NEW WAR.

Come to your heaven, you heavenly quires!Earth hath the heaven of your desires;Remove your dwelling to your God,A stall is now His blest abode;Sith men their homage do deny,Come, angels, all their fault supply.

This little Babe, so few days old,Is come to rifle Satan's fold;All hell doth at His presence quake,Though He himself for cold do shake;For in this weak, unarméd wiseThe gates of hell He will surprise.

My soul, with Christ join thou in fight;Stick to the tents that He hath pight;Within His crib is surest ward,This little Babe will be thy guard;If thou wilt foil thy foes with joy,Then flit not from this heavenly Boy.

Robert Southwell.

FOR CHRISTMAS DAY.

Rejoice, rejoice, with heart and voice!In Christé's birth this day rejoice!From Virgin's womb this day did springThe precious seed that only savéd man;This day let man rejoice and sweetly sing,Since on this day salvation first began.This day did Christ man's soul from death remove,With glorious saints to dwell in heaven above.

This day to man came pledge of perfect peace,This day to man came perfect unity,This day man's grief began for to surcease,This day did man receive a remedyFor each offence and every deadly sin,With guilty heart that erst he wandered in.

In Christé's flock let love be surely placed,From Christé's flock let concord hate expel,Of Christé's flock let love be so embracedAs we in Christ and Christ in us may dwell;Christ is the author of all unity,From whence proceedeth all felicity.

O sing unto this glittering, glorious king,O praise His name let every living thing;Let heart and voice, like bells of silver, ringThe comfort that this day doth bring;Let lute, let shawm, with sound of sweet delight,The joy of Christé's birth this day recite.

Francis Kinwelmersh, a.d. 1576.

SUNG TO THE KING IN THE PRESENCE AT WHITEHALL.

Chor.—What sweeter music can we bring,Than a carol for to singThe birth of this our heavenly King?Awake the voice! awake the string!Heart, ear, and eye, and everythingAwake! the while the active fingerRuns divisions with the singer.

From the flourish they come to the song.

Dark and dull night, fly hence away,And give the honor to this day,That sees December turn'd to May.

If we may ask the reason, sayThe why and wherefore all things hereSeem like the spring-time of the year?Why does the chilling winter's mornSmile like a field beset with corn?Or smell like to a mead new-shorn,Thus on the sudden? Come and seeThe cause why things thus fragrant be:'Tis He is born whose quickening birthGives life and lustre public mirthTo heaven and the under-earth.

Chor.—We see Him come, and know Him ours,Who with His sunshine and His showersTurns all the patient ground to flowers.

The darling of the world is come,And fit it is we find a roomTo welcome Him. The nobler partOf all the house here is the heart.

Chor.—Which we will give Him; and bequeathThis holly and this ivy wreath,To do Him honor, who's our King,And Lord of all this revelling.

Robert Herrick.

AND THEY LAID HIM IN A MANGER.

Happy crib, that wert aloneTo my God, bed, cradle, throne!Whilst thy glorious vileness IView with divine fancy's eye,Sordid filth seems all the cost,State, and splendor, crowns do boast.

See heaven's sacred majestyHumbled beneath poverty;Swaddled up in homely ragsOn a bed of straw and flags!He whose hands the heavens displayed,And the world's foundation laid,From the world's almost exiled,Of all ornaments despoiled.Perfumes bathe Him not, new-born,Persian mantles not adorn;Nor do the rich roofs look brightWith the jasper's orient light.Where, O royal Infant, beTh' ensigns of Thy majesty;Thy Sire's equalizing state;And Thy sceptre that rules fate?Where's Thy angel-guarded throne,Whence Thy laws Thou didst make known,Laws which heaven, earth, hell, obeyed?These, ah! these aside He laid;Would the emblem be—of prideBy humility outvied?

Sir Edward Sherburne.

THE BURNING BABE.

As I in hoary winter's night stood shivering in the snow,Surprised I was with sudden heat which made my heart to glow;And lifting up a fearful eye to view what fire was near,A pretty babe all burning bright did in the air appear,Who, scorchéd with excessive heat, such floods of tears did shed,As though his floods should quench his flames which with his tears were fed.Alas! quoth he, but newly born in fiery heats I fry,Yet none approach to warm their hearts or feel my fire but I.My faultless breast the furnace is, the fuel wounding thorns:Love is the fire and sighs the smoke, the ashes shame and scorns:The fuel justice layeth on, and mercy blows the coals;The metal in this furnace wrought are men's defiléd souls;For which, as now on fire I am, to work them to their good,So will I melt into a bath to wash them in my blood.With that he vanish'd out of sight and swiftly shrunk away.And straight I calléd unto mind that it was Christmas Day.

Robert Southwell.

CHRIST'S NATIVITY.

Awake, glad heart! get up and sing!It is the birthday of thy
King.Awake! awake!The sun doth shakeLight from his locks,
and, all the wayBreathing perfumes, doth spice the day.

Awake! awake! hark how th' wood rings,Winds whisper, and the
busy springsA concert make!Awake! awake!Man is their high-
priest, and should riseTo offer up the sacrifice.

I would I were some bird or starFluttering in woods, or lifted
farAbove this inn,And road of sin!Then either star or bird should
beShining or singing still to Thee.

I would I had in my best partFit rooms for Thee! or that my
heartWere so clean asThy manger was!But I am all filth, and
obscene;Yet, if Thou wilt, Thou canst make clean.

Sweet Jesu! will then. Let no moreThis leper haunt and soil Thy
door!Cure him, ease him,O release him!And let once more, by
mystic birth,The Lord of life be born in earth.

Henry Vaughan.

AN ODE ON THE BIRTH OF OUR SAVIOUR.

In numbers, and but these few, I sing Thy birth, O Jesu! Thou pretty baby, born here With sup'rabundant scorn here: Who, for Thy princely port here, Hadst for Thy place Of birth a base Out-stable for Thy court here.

Instead of neat enclosures Of interwoven osiers, Instead of fragrant posies Of daffodils and roses, Thy cradle, kingly stranger, As gospel tells, Was nothing else But here a homely manger.

But we with silks not crewels, With sundry precious jewels, And lily work will dress Thee; And, as we dispossess Thee Of clouts, we'll make a chamber, Sweet babe, for Thee Of ivory And plaster'd round with amber.

The Jews they did disdain Thee, But we will entertain Thee With glories to await here Upon Thy princely state here; And, more for love than pity, From year to year We'll make Thee here A free-born of our city.

Robert Herrick.

WHO CAN FORGET?

Who can forget—never to be forgot—The time, that all the world in slumber lies,When, like the stars, the singing angels shotTo earth, and heaven awaked all his eyesTo see another sun at midnight riseOn earth? Was never sight of pareil fameFor God before, man like himself did frame,But God himself now like a mortal man became.

A child He was, and had not learnt to speak,That with His word the world before did make;His mother's arms Him bore, He was so weak,That with one hand the vaults of heaven could shake;See how small room my infant Lord doth take,Whom all the world is not enough to hold!Who of His years or of His age hath told?Never such age so young, never a child so old.

And yet but newly He was infanted,And yet already He was sought to die;Yet scarcely born, already banished;Not able yet to go, and forced to fly:But scarcely fled away, when by and byThe tyrant's sword with blood is all defiled,And Rachel, for her sons, with fury wild,Cries, "O thou cruel king, and O my sweetest Child!"

Egypt His nurse became, where Nilus springs,Who, straight to entertain the rising sun,The hasty harvest in his bosom brings;But now for drought the fields were all undone,And now with waters all is overrun:So fast the Cynthian mountains pour'd their snow,When once they felt the sun so near them glow,That Nilus Egypt lost, and to a sea did grow.

The angels carolled loud their song of peace;The cursed oracles were strucken dumb;To see their Shepherd the poor shepherds press;To see their King, the kingly sophies[S] come;And them to guide unto his Master's home,A star comes dancing up the orient,That springs for joy over the strawy tent,Where gold, to make their prince a crown, they all present.

Giles Fletcher.

FOOTNOTE:

[S]Wise men.

THE CHILD JESUS.

A CORNISH CAROL.

Welcome that star in Judah's sky, That voice o'er Bethlehem's palmy glen! The lamp far sages hailed on high, The tones that thrilled the shepherd men: Glory to God in loftiest heaven! Thus angels smote the echoing chord; Glad tidings unto man forgiven, Peace from the presence of the Lord.

The Shepherds sought that birth divine, The Wise Men traced their guided way; There, by strange light and mystic sign, The God they came to worship lay. A human Babe in beauty smiled, Where lowing oxen round Him trod: A maiden clasped her awful Child, Pure offspring of the breath of God.

Those voices from on high are mute, The star the Wise Men saw is dim; But hope still guides the wanderer's foot, And faith renews the angel hymn: Glory to God in loftiest heaven! Touch with glad hand the ancient chord; Good tidings unto man forgiven, Peace from the presence of the Lord.

Robert Stephen Hawker.

LONG AGO.

In the bleak mid-winterFrosty wind made moan,Earth stood hard as iron,Water like a stone;Snow had fallen, snow on snow,Snow on snow,In the bleak mid-winterLong ago.

Our God, heaven cannot hold Him,Nor earth sustain;Heaven and earth shall flee awayWhen He comes to reign:In the bleak mid-winterA stable-place sufficedThe Lord God Almighty,Jesus Christ.

Enough for Him whom cherubimWorship night and day,A breastful of milkAnd a mangerful of hay;Enough for Him whom angelsFall down before,The ox and ass and camelWhich adore.

Angels and archangelsMay have gathered there,Cherubim and seraphimThronged the air;But only His mother,In her maiden bliss,Worshipped the BelovedWith a kiss.

What can I give Him,Poor as I am?If I were a shepherd,I would bring a lamb;If I were a wise man,I would do my part:Yet what I can I give Him,Give my heart.

Christina G. Rossetti.

"What Can I Give Him?"

STAR OF BETHLEHEM.

When marshalled on the nightly plainThe glitt'ring host bestud the sky,One star alone of all the trainCan fix the sinner's wandering eye.Hark! hark! to God the chorus breaksFrom ev'ry host, from ev'ry gem;But one alone the Saviour speaks,—It is the Star of Bethlehem!

Once on the raging seas I rode;The storm was loud, the night was dark;The ocean yawned, and rudely blewThe wind that tossed my found'ring bark.Deep horror then my vitals froze;Death-struck, I ceased the tide to stem,When suddenly a star arose,—It was the Star of Bethlehem!

It was my guide, my light, my all;It bade my dark forebodings cease;And through the storm and danger's thrall,It led me to the port of peace.Now safely moored, my perils o'er,I'll sing first in night's diadem,Forever and forever more,—The Star, the Star of Bethlehem!

Henry Kirke White.

NO ROOM.

Foot-sore and weary, Mary triedSome rest to seek, but was denied."There is no room," the blind ones cried.

Meekly the Virgin turned away,No voice entreating her to stay;There was no room for God that day.

No room for her, round whose tired feetAngels are bowed in transport sweetThe mother of their God to greet.

No room for Him in whose small handThe troubled sea and mighty landLie cradled like a grain of sand;

No room, O Babe Divine! for TheeThat Christmas night; and even weDare shut our hearts and turn the key.

In vain Thy pleading baby cryStrikes our deaf souls; we pass Thee by,Unsheltered 'neath the wintry sky.

No room for God! O Christ, that weShould bar our doors, nor ever seeOur Saviour waiting patiently.

Fling wide the doors! Dear Christ, turn back!The ashes on my hearth lie black—Of light and warmth a total lack.

How can I bid Thee enter hereAmid the desolation drearOf lukewarm love and craven fear?

What bleaker shelter can there beThan my cold heart's tepidity—Chilled, wind-tossed, as the winter sea?

Dear Lord, I shrink from Thy pure eye, No home to offer Thee have I; Yet in Thy mercy pass not by.

Agnes Repplier.

ON CHRISTMAS DAY.

Assist me, Muse divine! to Sing the MornOn which the Saviour of Mankind was born;But oh! what Numbers to the Theme can rise?Unless kind Angels aid me from the Skies!Methinks I see the tunefull Host descend,And with officious Joy the Scene attend!Hark, by their Hymns directed on the Road,The Gladsome Shepherds find the nascent God!And view the Infant conscious of his Birth,Smiling bespeak Salvation to the Earth!For when th' important Æra first drew nearIn which the great Messiah should appear;And to accomplish his redeeming Love;Beneath our Form should every Woe sustain,And by triumphant Suffering fix his Reign,Should for lost Man in Tortures yield his BreathDying to save us from eternal Death!Oh mystick union!—salutary Grace!Incarnate God our Nature should embrace!That Deity should stoop to our Disguise!That man recover'd should regain the Skies!Dejected Adam! from thy grave ascend,And view the Serpent's Deadly Malice end,   Adorning bless th' Almighty's boundless GraceThat gave his son a Ransome for thy Race!Oh never let my Soul this Day forget,But pay in gratefull praise the annual Debt.

From a manuscript volume, written by George Washington.

71

THE HEAVENLY CHOIR.

What sudden blaze of songSpreads o'er th' expanse of heaven?In waves of light it thrills along,Th' angelic signal given—"Glory to God!" from yonder central fireFlows out the echoing lay beyond the starry quire;

Like circles widening roundUpon a clear blue river,Orb after orb, the wondrous soundIs echoed on forever;"Glory to God on high, on earth be peace,And love toward men of love—salvation and release."

Yet stay, before thou dareTo join that festal throng;Listen and mark what gentle airFirst stirred the tide of song;'Tis not, "the Saviour born in David's home,To whom for power and health obedient worlds should come:"

'Tis not "the Christ the Lord:"—With fix'd adoring lookThe choir of angels caught the word,Nor yet their silence broke;But when they heard the sign, where Christ should be,In sudden light they shone and heavenly harmony.

Wrapped in His swaddling-bands,And in His manger laid,The hope and glory of all landsIs come to the world's aid:No peaceful home upon His cradle smiled,Guests rudely went and came where slept the royal Child.

But where Thou dwellest, Lord,No other thought should be;Once duly welcomed and adored,How should I part with Thee?Bethlehem must lose Thee soon, but Thou wilt graceThe single heart to be Thy pure abiding-place.

Thee, on the bosom laidOf a pure virgin mind,In quiet ever, and in shade,Shepherd and sage may find; They who have bow'd untaught to nature's sway,And they who follow truth along her star-paved way.

The pastoral spirits firstApproach Thee, Babe divine,For they in lowly thoughts are nursed,Meet for Thy lowly shrine:Sooner than they should miss where Thou dost dwell,Angels from heaven will stoop to guide them to Thy cell.

Still, as the day comes roundFor Thee to be revealed,By wakeful shepherds Thou art found,Abiding in the field.All through the wintry heaven and chill night air,In music and in light Thou dawnest on their prayer.

O faint not ye for fear—What though your wandering sheep,Reckless of what they see and hear,Lie lost in wilful sleep?High heaven in mercy to your sad annoyStill greets you with glad tidings of immortal joy.

Think on th' eternal homeThe Saviour left for you;Think on the Lord most holy, comeTo dwell with hearts untrue:So shall ye tread untired His pastoral ways,And in the darkness sing your carol of high praise.

John Keble.

The Wassail-Bowl.

"Wassail, wassail, all over the town;Our toast it is white, our ale it is brown,Our bowl it is made of the mapling tree;With the wassailing bowl we will drink to thee."

Old Carol.

WASSAIL.

Give way, give way, ye gates, and winAn easy blessing to your binAnd basket, by our entering in.

May both with manchet[T] stand replete, Your larders, too, so hung with meat, That though a thousand thousand eat,

Yet ere twelve moons shall whirl aboutTheir silvery spheres, there's none may doubtBut more's sent in than was served out.

Next, may your dairies prosper soAs that your pans no ebb may know;But if they do, the more to flow,

Like to a solemn, sober stream, Banked all with lilies, and the creamOf sweetest cowslips filling them.

Then may your plants be pressed with fruit, Nor bee or hive you have be mute, But sweetly sounding like a lute.

Last, may your harrows, shares, and ploughs, Your stacks, your stocks, your sweetest mows, All prosper by your virgin vows.

Alas! we bless, but see none here, That brings us either ale or beer;In a dry house all things are near.

Let's leave a longer time to wait, Where rust and cobwebs bind the gate;And all live here with needy fate;

Where chimneys do forever weepFor want of warmth, and stomachs keepWith noise the servants' eyes from sleep.

It is in vain to sing or stayOur free feet here, but we'll away;Yet to the Lares this we'll say:

The time will come when you'll be sad,And reckon this for fortune bad,T' have lost the good ye might have had.

Robert Herrick.

FOOTNOTE:

[T]White bread.

INVITATION À FAIRE NOËL.

(FROM THE FRENCH OF THE TWELFTH CENTURY.)

Hail, good Masters, let us bide,Hither come from travel wide,This Christmas-tide.Hearken, give us bed and cheer,We are weary, life is dearThis day o' the year!God send ye joy and peace on earth,Who broach good cheer for Christé's birth.

Masters, an ye make no feast:Spicéd ale and meat of beast,Nor laugh the least:If ye fill not pantries highWith bread, and fish, and mammoth pie,And sweets, pardie!—God ordains no peace on earthTo ye who fast at Christé's birth.

Masters, it is writ of oldWho fill the fire for Christmas coldAnd wassail hold,Shall have of food a double storeAnd ruddy-blazing ingle roarForevermore. God sends the peace of heaven and earthTo men who carol Christé's birth.

O Masters! let nor hate nor spiteMar the tongue of any wight'Twixt night and night.Botun, batun—belabor wellChurls who sleep through matin bellAnd no soothe tell.God will forfeit peace on earthIf men fall out at Christé's birth.

Christmas tipples every wine,English, French, and Gascon fineAnd Angevine;Clinks with neighbor and with guest,Empties casks with gibe and jest—The year's for rest!God sends to men the joy of earthWho broach good cheer for Christé's birth.

But hearken, Masters, ere ye drinkWhile yet the bubbles boil and winkAt the brink;Ere ye lift the pot aloft,Merrily wave it, laughing oft,With hood well doft.And if I cry ye, sad, "Wesseyl!"Woe's him who answers not "Drinchayl!"

Translated by H. S. M.

A THANKSGIVING.

Lord, I confess too, when I dine,The pulse is Thine,And all those other bits that beThere placed by Thee;The worts, the purslane, and the messOf water-cress,Which of Thy kindness Thou hast sent;And my contentMakes those and my belovéd beetTo be more sweet.'Tis Thou that crown'st my glittering hearthWith guiltless mirth,And giv'st me wassail-bowls to drinkSpiced to the brink.

Robert Herrick.

AROUND THE WASSAIL-BOWL.

A jolly wassail-bowl, A wassail of good ale; Well fare the butler's soul That setteth this to sale; Our jolly wassail.

Good dame, here at your door Our wassail we begin, We are all maidens poor, We pray now let us in With our wassail.

Our wassail we do fill With apples and with spice, Then grant us your good-will To taste here once or twice Of our good wassail.

If any maidens be Here dwelling in this house, They kindly will agree To take a full carouse Of our wassail.

But here they let us stand All freezing in the cold: Good master, give command To enter and be bold, With our wassail.

Much joy into this hall With us is entered in, Our master first of all We hope will now begin Of our wassail.

And after, his good wife Our spicéd bowl will try; The Lord prolong your life! Good fortune we espy For our wassail.

Some bounty from your hands Our wassail to maintain; We'll buy no house nor lands With that which we do gain With our wassail.

This is our merry night Of choosing king and queen; Then be it your delight That something may be seen In our wassail.

It is a noble partTo bear a liberal mind;God bless our master's heart!For here we comfort findWith our wassail.

And now we must be goneTo seek out more good cheer,Where bounty will be shownAs we have found it hereWith our wassail.

Much joy betide them all,Our prayer shall be still,We hope and ever shallFor this your great good-willTo our wassail.

FROM DOOR TO DOOR.

Here we come a wassailingAmong the leaves so green,Here we come a wand'ring,So fair to be seen.Love and joy come to you,And to you your wassail too,And God bless you and send you a happy New Year.

Our wassail-cup is madeOf the rosemary tree,And so is your beerOf the best barley.Love and joy, etc.

We are not daily beggarsThat beg from door to door,But we are neighbors' childrenWhom you have seen before.Love and joy, etc.

Good master and good mistress,As you sit by the fire,Pray think of us poor childrenAs wand'ring in the mire.Love and joy, etc.

We have a little purseMade of ratching leather skin;We want some of your small changeTo line it well within.Love and joy, etc.

Call up the butler of this house,Put on his golden ring;Let him bring us a glass of beer,And the better we shall sing.Love and joy, etc.

Bring us out a table,And spread it with a cloth;Bring us out a mouldy cheese,And some of your Christmas loaf.Love and joy, etc.

God bless the master of this house,Likewise the mistress tooAnd all the little childrenThat round the table go.Love and joy, etc.

WASSAILING CAROL.

We wish you merry Christmas, also a glad New Year;We come to bring you tidings to all mankind so dear:We come to tell that Jesus was born in Bethl'em town,And now He's gone to glory and pityingly looks downOn us poor wassailers,As wassailing we go;With footsteps soreFrom door to doorWe trudge through sleet and snow.

A manger was His cradle, the straw it was His bed,The oxen were around Him within that lowly shed;No servants waited on Him with lords and ladies gay;But now He's gone to glory and unto Him we pray.Us poor wassailers, etc.

His mother loved and tended Him and nursed Him at her breast,And good old Joseph watched them both the while they took their rest;And wicked Herod vainly sought to rob them of their child,By slaughtering the Innocents in Bethlehem undefiled.But us poor wassailers, etc.

Now, all good Christian people, with great concern we singThese tidings of your Jesus, the Saviour, Lord and King;In poverty He passed His days that riches we might share,And of your wealth He bids you give and of your portion spareTo us poor wassailers, etc.

Your wife shall be a fruitful vine, a hus'sif good and able;Your children like the olive branches round about your table;Your barns shall burst with plenty and your crops shall be secure,If you will give your charity to us who are so poor,Us poor wassailers, etc.

And now no more we'll sing to you because the hour is late,And we must trudge and sing our song at many another gate;And so we'll wish you once again a merry Christmas time,And pray God bless you while you give good silver for our rhyme.Us poor wassailers, etc.

A CAROL AT THE GATES.

Here we come a-whistling through the fields so green; Here we come a-singing, so fair to be seen. God send you happy, God send you happy, Pray God send you a happy New Year!

The roads are very dirty, my boots are very thin, I have a little pocket to put a penny in. God send you happy, etc.

Bring out your little table and spread it with a cloth, Bring out some of your old ale, likewise your Christmas loaf. God send you happy, etc.

God bless the master of this house, likewise the mistress, too, And all the little children that round the table strew. God send you happy, etc.

The cock sat up in the yew-tree, the hen came chuckling by, I wish you a merry Christmas, and a good fat pig in the sty. God send you happy, etc.

WANDERING WASSAILERS.

Wassail, wassail, all over the town,Our bread it is white, and our ale it is brown;Our bowl it is made of the maplin tree,So here, my good fellow, I'll drink it to thee.

The wassailing bowl, with a toast within,Come, fill it up unto the brim;Come fill it up that we may all see;With the wassailing bowl I'll drink to thee.

Come, butler, come bring us a bowl of your best,And we hope your soul in heaven shall rest;But if you do bring us a bowl of your small,Then down shall go butler, the bowl, and all.

O butler, O butler, now don't you be worst,But pull out your knife and cut us a toast;And cut us a toast, one that we may all see;With the wassailing bowl I'll drink to thee.

Here's to Dobbin and to his right eye!God send our mistress a good Christmas-pie!A good Christmas-pie as e'er we did see;With the wassailing bowl I'll drink to thee.

Here's to Broad May and his broad horn,God send our master a good crop of corn,A good crop of corn as we all may see;With the wassailing bowl I'll drink to thee.

Here's to Colly and to her long tail,We hope our master and mistress heart will ne'er fail;But bring us a bowl of your good strong beer,And then we shall taste of your happy New Year.

Be there here any pretty maids? we hope there be some;Don't let the jolly wassailers stand on the cold stone,But open the door and pull out the pin,That we jolly wassailers may all sail in.

Chappell's Ancient English Melodies.

BRING US IN GOOD ALE.

Bring us in good ale, and bring us in good ale;For our blessed Lady's sake, bring us in good ale.

Bring us in no brown bread, for that is made of bran,Nor bring us in no white bread, for therein is no game,But bring us in good ale.

Bring us in no beef, for there are many bones,But bring us in good ale, for that goeth down at once;And bring us in good ale.

Bring us in no bacon, for that is passing fat,But bring us in good ale, and give us enough of that;And bring us in good ale.

Bring us in no mutton, for that is often lean,Nor bring us in no tripes, for they be seldom clean;But bring us in good ale.

Bring us in no eggs, for there are many shells,But bring us in good ale, and give us nothing else;And bring us in good ale.

Bring us in no butter, for therein are many hairs,Nor bring us in no pig's flesh, for that will make us boars;But bring us in good ale.

Bring us in no puddings, for therein is all God's good,Nor bring us in no venison, for that is not for our blood;But bring us in good ale.

Bring us in no capon's flesh, for that is often dear,Nor bring us in no duck's flesh, for they slobber in the mere;But bring us in good ale.

Wright's Songs and Carols.

ABOUT THE BOARD.

Come bravely on, my masters,For here we shall be tastersOf curious dishes that are brave and fine,Where they that do such cheer afford,I'll lay my knife upon the board,My master and my dame they do not pine.

Who is't will not be merryAnd sing down, down, aderry?For now it is a time of joy and mirth;'Tis said 'tis merry in the hallWhen as beards they do wag all;God's plenty's here, it doth not show a dearth.

Let him take all lives longest,Come fill us of the strongest,And I will drink a health to honest John;Come, pray thee, butler, fill the bowl,And let it round the table troll,When that is up, I'll tell you more anon.

New Christmas Carols, a.d. 1642.

___

BEFORE THE FEAST.

All you that are good fellows,Come hearken to my song;I know you do not hate good cheerNor liquor that is strong.I hope there is none hereBut soon will take my part,Seeing my master and my dameSay welcome with their heart.

This is a time of joyfulnessAnd merry time of year,Whereas the rich with plenty storedDoth make the poor good cheer;Plum-porridge, roast-beef, and minced-piesStand smoking on the board,With other brave varietiesOur master doth afford.

Our mistress and her cleanly maidsHave neatly played the cooks;Methinks these dishes eagerlyAt my sharp stomach looks,As though they were afraidTo see me draw my blade;But I revenged on them will beUntil my stomach's stayed.

Come fill us of the strongest,Small drink is out of date;Methinks I shall fare like a princeAnd sit in gallant state:This is no miser's feast,Although that things be dear;God grant the founder of this feastEach Christmas keep good cheer.

This day for Christ we celebrate,Who was born at this time;For which all Christians should rejoice,And I do sing in rhyme.When you have given God thanks,Unto your dainties fall:Heaven bless my master and my dame,Lord bless me and you all.

New Christmas Carols, a.d. 1642.

A BILL OF CHRISTMAS FARE.

Come, mad boys, be glad, boys, for Christmas is here, And we shall be feasted with jolly good cheer; Then let us be merry, 'tis Saint Stephen's day, Let's eat and drink freely, here's nothing to pay.

My master bids welcome, and so doth my dame, And 'tis yonder smoking dish doth me inflame; Anon I'll be with you, though you me outface, For now I do tell you I have time and place.

I'll troll the bowl to you, then let it go round, My heels are so light they can stand on no ground; My tongue it doth chatter, and goes pitter patter, Here's good beer and strong beer, for I will not flatter.

And now for remembrance of blessed Saint Stephen, Let's joy at morning, at noon, and at even; Then leave off your mincing, and fall to mince-pies, I pray take my counsel, be ruled by the wise.

New Christmas Carols, a.d. 1642.

THE MAHOGANY-TREE.

Christmas is here:Winds whistle shrill,Icy and chill,Little care we:Little we fearWeather withoutSheltered aboutThe Mahogany-Tree.

Once on the boughsBirds of rare plumeSang, in its bloom;Night-birds are we:Here we carouse,Singing like them,Perched round the stemOf the jolly old tree.

Here let us sport,Boys, as we sit;Laughter and witFlashing so free,Life is but short—When we are gone, Let them sing onRound the old tree.

Evenings we knew,Happy as this;Faces we miss,Pleasant to see,Kind hearts and true,Gentle and just,Peace to your dust,We sing round the tree.

Care, like a dun,Lurks at the gate:Let the dog wait;Happy we'll be!Drink, every one;Pile up the coals,Fill the red bowls,Round the old tree!

Drain we the cup—Friend, art afraid?Spirits are laidIn the Red Sea.Mantle it up;Empty it yet;Let us forget,Round the old tree.

Sorrow, begone!Life and its ills,Duns and their bills,Bid we to flee.Come with the dawn,Blue-devil sprite,Leave us to-nightRound the old tree.

William Makepeace Thackeray.

A CHRISTMAS CEREMONY.

Wassail the trees, that they may bearYou many a plum and many a pear;For more or less fruits they will bringAs you do give them wassailing.

Robert Herrick.

WITH CAKES AND ALE.

With cakes and ale, and antic ringWell tiptoed to the tabor string,And many a buss below the holly,And flout at sable melancholy—So, with a rouse, went Christmassing!

What! are no latter waits to sing?No clog to blaze? No wit to wing?Are catches gone, and dimpled Dolly,With cakes and ale?

Nay, an you will, behold the thing:The spicéd meat, the minstreling!Undo Misrule, and many a volleyOf losel snatches born of folly—Bring back the cheer, be Christmas-king,With cakes and ale!

H. S. M.

THE MASQUE OF CHRISTMAS.

(AS IT WAS PRESENTED AT COURT, 1616.)

The Court being seated,

Enter Christmas, with two or three of the guard, attired in round hose, long stockings, a close doublet, a high-crowned hat, with a brooch, a long, thin beard, a truncheon, little ruffs, white shoes, his scarfs and garters tied cross, and his drum beaten before him.

Why, gentlemen, do you know what you do? ha! would you have kept me out? Christmas, old Christmas, Christmas of London, and Captain Christmas? Pray you, let me be brought before my lord chamberlain, I'll not be answered else: *'Tis merry in hall, when beards wag all:* I have seen the time you have wish'd for me for a merry Christmas; and now you have me, they would not let me in: *I must come another time!* a good jest, as if I could come more than once a year! Why, I am no dangerous person, and so I told my friends of the guard. I am old Gregory Christmas still, and though I come out of Pope's-head alley, as good a Protestant as any in my parish. The truth is, I have brought a Masque here, out o' the city, of my own making, and do present it by a set of my sons, that come out of the lanes of London, good dancing boys all. It was intended, I confess, for Curriers Hall; but because the weather has been open, and the Livery were not at leisure to see it till a frost came, that they cannot work, I thought it convenient, with some little alterations, and the groom of the revels' hand to 't, to fit it for a higher place; which I have done, and though I say it, another manner of device than your New-Year's-night. Bones o' bread, the king! (*seeing King James.*) Son Rowland! Son Clem! be ready there in a trice: quick, boys!

Enter his Sons and Daughters, (ten in number,) led in, in a string, by Cupid, who is attired in a flat cap, and a prentice's coat, with wings at his shoulders.

Misrule, in a velvet cap, with a sprig, a short cloak, great yellow ruff, like a reveller, his torch-bearer bearing a rope, a cheese, and a basket.

Carol, a long tawny coat, with a red cap, and a flute at his girdle, his torch-bearer carrying a song-book open.

Minced-Pie, like a fine cook's wife, drest neat; her man carrying a pie, dish, and spoons.

Gambol, like a tumbler, with a hoop and bells; his torch-bearer armed with a colt-staff, and a binding cloth.

Post and Pair, with a pair-royal of aces in his hat; his garment all done over with pairs and purs; his squire carrying a box, cards, and counters.

New-Year's-Gift, in a blue coat, serving-man like, with an orange, and a sprig of rosemary gilt on his head, his hat full of brooches, with a collar of ginger-bread, his torch-bearer carrying a march-pane with a bottle of wine on either arm.

Mumming, in a masquing pied suit, with a vizard, his torch-bearer carrying the box, and ringing it.

Wassel, like a neat sempster and songster; her page bearing a brown bowl, drest with ribands, and rosemary before her.

Offering, in a short gown, with a porter's staff in his hand, a wyth born before him, and a bason, by his torch-bearer.

Baby-Cake, drest like a boy, in a fine long coat, biggin-bib, muckender, and a little dagger; his usher bearing a great cake, with a bean and a pease.

They enter singing.

Now God preserve, as you do well deserve, Your majesties all, two there; Your highness small, with my good lords all, And ladies, how do you do there?

Give me leave to ask, for I bring you a masque From little, little, little London; Which say the king likes, I have passed the pikes, If not, old Christmas is undone.

[*Noise without.*

Chris. Ho, peace! what's the matter there?

Gam. Here's one o' Friday-street would come in.

Chris. By no means, nor out of neither of the Fish-streets, admit not a man; they are not Christmas creatures: fish and fasting days, foh! Sons, said I well? look to it.

Gam. No body out o' Friday-street, nor the two Fish-streets there, do you hear?

Car. Shall John Butter o' Milk-street come in? Ask him.

Gam. Yes, he may slip in for a torch-bearer, so he melt not too fast, that he will last till the masque be done.

Chris. Right, son.

Our dance's freight is a matter of eight;And two, the which are wenches:In all they be ten, four cocks to a hen,And will swim to the tune like tenches.

Each hath his knight for to carry his light,Which some would say are torchesTo bring them here, and to lead them there,And home again to their own porches.

Now their intent,—

Enter Venus, *a deaf tire-woman.*

Ven. Now, all the lords bless me! where am I, trow? where is Cupid? "Serve the king!" they may serve the cobbler well enough, some of 'em, for any courtesy they have, I wisse; they have need o' mending: unrude people they are, your courtiers; here was thrust upon thrust indeed: was it ever so hard to get in before, trow?

Chris. How now? what's the matter?

Ven. A place, forsooth, I do want a place: I would have a good place, to see my child act in before the king and queen's majesties, God bless 'em! to-night.

Chris. Why, here is no place for you.

Ven. Right, forsooth, I am Cupid's mother, Cupid's own mother, forsooth; yes, forsooth: I dwell in Pudding-lane: ay, forsooth, he is prentice in Love-lane, with a bugle maker, that makes of your bobs, and bird-bolts for ladies.

Chris. Good lady Venus of Pudding-lane, you must go out for all this.

Ven. Yes, forsooth, I can sit anywhere, so I may see Cupid act: he is a pretty child, though I say it, that perhaps should not, you will say. I had him by my first husband; he was a smith, forsooth, we dwelt in Do-little-lane then: he came a month before his time, and that may make him somewhat imperfect; but I was a fishmonger's daughter.

Chris. No matter for your pedigree, your house: good Venus, will you depart?

Ven. Ay, forsooth, he'll say his part, I warrant him, as well as e'er a play-boy of 'em all: I could have had money enough for him, an I would have been tempted, and have let him out by the week to the king's players. Master Burbage has been about and about with me, and so has old master Hemings, too, they have need of him; where is he, trow, ha! I would fain see him—pray God they have given him some drink since he came.

Chris. Are you ready, boys? Strike up! nothing will drown this noise but a drum: a'peace, yet! I have not done. Sing,—

Now their intent is above to present—

Car. Why, here be half of the properties forgotten, father.

Offer. Post and Pair wants his pur-chops and his pur-dogs.

Car. Have you ne'er a son at the groom porter's, to beg or borrow a pair of cards quickly?

Gam. It shall not need; here's your son Cheater without, has cards in his pocket.

Offer. Ods so! speak to the guards to let him in, under the name of a property.

Gam. And here's New-Year's-Gift has an orange and rosemary, but not a clove to stick in't.

New-Year. Why, let one go to the spicery.

Chris. Fy, fy, fy! it's naught, it's naught, boys.

Ven. Why, I have cloves, if it be cloves you want. I have cloves in my purse: I never go without one in my mouth.

Car. And Mumming has not his vizard, neither.

Chris. No matter! his own face shall serve, for a punishment, and 'tis bad enough; has Wassel her bowl, and Minced-pie her spoons?

Offer. Ay, ay: but Misrule doth not like his suit: he says the players have sent him one too little, on purpose to disgrace him.

Chris. Let him hold his peace, and his disgrace will be the less: what! shall we proclaim where we were furnish'd? Mum! mum! a'peace! be ready, good boys.

Now their intent is above to present, With all the appurtenances, A right Christmas, as of old it was, To be gathered out of the dances.

Which they do bring, and afore the king, The queen, and prince, as it were now Drawn here by love; who over and above, Doth draw himself in the geer too.

Here the drum and fife sound, and they march about once. In the second coming up, Christmas proceeds in his song:

Hum drum, sauce for a coney; No more of your martial music; Even for the sake o' the next new stake, For there I do mean to use it.

And now to ye, who in place are to see With roll and farthingale hoopéd: I pray you know, though he want his bow, By the wings, that this is Cupid.

He might go back for to cry, *What you lack?* But that were not so witty: His cap and coat are enough to note That he is the love o' the city.

And he leads on, though he now be gone, For that was only his-rule: But now comes in, Tom of Bosoms-inn, And he presenteth Mis-rule.

Which you may know, by the very show, Albeit you never ask it: For there you may see what his ensigns be, The rope, the cheese, and the basket.

This Carol plays, and has been in his daysA chirping boy, and a kill-pot:Kit Cobler it is, I'm a father of his,And he dwells in a lane called Fill-pot.

But who is this? O, my daughter Cis,Minced-pie; with her do not dallyOn pain o' your life: she's an honest cook's wife,And comes out of Scalding-alley.

Next in the trace, comes Gambol in place;And, to make my tale the shorter,My son Hercules, tane out of Distaff-lane,But an active man, and a porter.

Now Post and Pair, old Christmas's heir,Doth make and a gingling sally;And wot you who, 'tis one of my twoSons, card-makers in Pur-alley.

Next in a trice, with his box and his dice,Mac-pipin my son, but younger,Brings Mumming in; and the knave will win,For he is a costermonger.

But New-Year's-Gift, of himself makes shift,To tell you what his name is:With orange on head, and his ginger-bread,Clem Waspe of Honey-lane 'tis.

This, I tell you, is our jolly Wassel,And for Twelfth-night more meet too:She works by the ell, and her name is Nell,And she dwells in Threadneedle-street too.

Then Offering, he, with his dish and his tree,That in every great house keepeth,Is by my son, young Little-worth, done,And in Penny-rich street he sleepeth.

Last, Baby-cake that an end doth makeOf Christmas, merry, merry vein-a,Is child Rowlan, and a straight young man,Though he come out of Crooked-lane-a.

There should have been, and a dozen I ween,But I could find but one moreChild of Christmas, and a Log it was,When I them all had gone o'er.

I prayed him, in a time so trim,That he would make one to prance it;And I myself would have been the twelfthO' but Log he was too heavy to dance it.

Now, Cupid, come you on.

Cup. You worthy wights, king, lords, and knights,
Or queen and ladies bright:
Cupid invites you to the sights
He shall present to-night.

Ven. 'Tis a good child, speak out; hold up your head, Love.

Cup. And which Cupid—and which Cupid—

Ven. Do not shake so, Robin; if thou be'st a-cold, I have some warm waters for thee here.

Chris. Come, you put Robin Cupid out with your water's and your fisling; will you be gone?

Ven. Ay, forsooth, he's a child, you must conceive, and must be used tenderly; he was never in such an assembly before, forsooth, but once at the Warmoll Quest, forsooth, where he said grace as prettily as any of the sheriff's hinch-boys, forsooth.

Chris. Will you peace, forsooth?

Cup. And which Cupid—and which Cupid—

Ven. Ay, that's a good boy, speak plain, Robin; how does his majesty like him, I pray? will he give eight-pence a day, think you? Speak out, Robin.

Chris. Nay, he is out enough. You may take him away, and begin your dance; this it is to have speeches.

Ven. You wrong the child, you do wrong the infant; I 'peal to his majesty.

Here they dance.

Chris. Well done, boys, my fine boys, my bully boys!

THE EPILOGUE.

Sings. Nor do you think that their legs is all
The commendation of my sons,
For at the Artillery garden they shall
As well forsooth use their guns,

And march as fine as the Muses nine,
Along the streets of London;
And in their brave tires, to give their false fires,
Especially Tom my son.

Now if the lanes and the allies afford
Such an ac-ativity as this;
At Christmas next, if they keep their word,
Can the children of Cheapside miss?

Though, put the case, when they come in place,
They should not dance, but hop: Their very gold lace, with their
silk, would 'em grace,
Having so many knights o' the shop.

But were I so wise, I might seem to advise
So great a potentate as yourself;
They should, sir, I tell ye, spare't out of their belly,
And this way spend some of their pelf.

Ay, and come to the court, for to make you some sport,

At the least once every year,
As Christmas hath done, with his seventh or eighth son,
And his couple of daughters dear.

And thus it ended.

Ben Jonson.

Santa Claus.

"His back, or rather burden showedAs if it stooped with its own load.To poise this, equally he boreA paunch of the same bulk before,Which still he had a special careTo keep well crammed with thrifty fare."

Butler.

A VISIT FROM ST. NICHOLAS.

'Twas the night before Christmas, when all through the houseNot a creature was stirring, not even a mouse;The stockings were hung by the chimney with care,In hopes that St. Nicholas soon would be there.The children were nestled all snug in their beds,While visions of sugar-plums danced in their heads;And mamma in her kerchief and I in my capHad just settled our brains for a long winter's nap,When out on the lawn there arose such a clatter,I sprang from my bed to see what was the matter.Away to the window I flew like a flash,Tore open the shutters and threw up the sash;The moon on the breast of the new-fallen snowGave the lustre of day to the objects below;When what to my wondering eyes should appearBut a miniature sleigh and eight tiny reindeer,With a little old driver so lively and quickI knew in a moment it must be St. Nick. More rapid than eagles, his coursers they came,And he whistled and shouted and called them by name:"Now, Dasher! now, Dancer! now, Prancer! now, Vixen!On, Comet! on, Cupid! on, Dunder and Blixen!To the top of the stoop, to the top of the wall!Now dash away! dash away! dash away all!"As dry leaves before the wild hurricane fly,When they meet with an obstacle, mount to the sky,So up to the house-top the coursers they flew,With the sleigh full of toys and St. Nicholas too;And then in a twinkling I heard on the roofThe prancing and pawing of each little hoof.As I drew in my head and was turning around,Down the chimney St. Nicholas came with a bound;He was dressed all in furs from his head to his foot,And his clothes were all tarnished with ashes and soot.A bundle of toys he had flung on his back;And he looked like a pedler just opening his pack.His eyes, how they twinkled! his dimples, how merry!His cheeks were like roses, his nose like a cherry; His droll little mouth was drawn up like a bow,And the beard on his chin was as white as the snow.The stump of a pipe he held tight in his teeth,And the smoke, it encircled his head like a wreath.He had a broad face, and a little round bellyThat shook when he laughed, like a bowl full of jelly.He was chubby and plump, a right jolly old elf,And I laughed when I saw him, in spite of myself.A wink of his eye and a twist of his headSoon gave me to know I had nothing to dread.He spoke not a word, but went straight to his work,And filled all the stockings, then turned with a jerk,And laying his finger aside of his nose,And giving a nod, up the chimney he rose.He sprang to his sleigh, to his team gave a whistle,And away they all flew like the down of a thistle;But I heard him exclaim, ere he drove out of sight,"Happy Christmas to all, and to all a good-night!"

Clement C. Moore.

THE HARD TIMES IN ELFLAND.

Strange that the termagant winds should scoldThe Christmas Eve so bitterly!But Wife, and Harry, the four-year old,Big Charley, Nimblewits, and I,

Blithe as the wind was bitter, drewMore frontward of the mighty fire,Where wise Newfoundland Fan foreknewThe heaven that Christian dogs desire—

Stretched o'er the rug, serene and grave,Huge nose on heavy paws reclined,With never a drowning boy to save,And warmth of body and peace of mind.

And as our happy circle sat,The fire well capp'd the company:In grave debate or careless chat,A right good fellow, mingled he:

He seemed as one of us to sit,And talked of things above, below,With flames more winsome than our wit,And coals that burned like love aglow.

While thus our rippling discourse rolledSmooth down the channel of the night,We spoke of Time: thereat, one toldA parable of the seasons' flight.

Those seasons out, we talked of these:And I, with inward purpose sly,To shield my purse from Christmas-trees,And stockings, and wild robbery

When Hal and Nimblewits invadeMy cash in Santa Claus's name,—In full the hard, hard times surveyed,Denounced all waste as crime and shame;

Hinted that "waste" might be a termIncluding skates, velocipedes,Kites, marbles, soldiers, towers infirm,Bows, arrows, cannon, Indian reeds,

Cap-pistols, drums, mechanic toys,And all th' infernal host of hornsWhereby to strenuous hells of noiseAre turned the blessed Christmas morns;

Thus, roused—those horns! to sacred rage,I rose, forefinger high in air,When Harry cried, some war to wage,"Papa is hard times ev'ywhere?

"Maybe in Santa Claus's landIt isn't hard times none at all!"Now, blessed vision! to my handMost pat, a marvel strange did fall.

Scarce had my Harry ceased, when "Look!"He cried, leapt up in wild alarm,Ran to my Comrade, shelter tookBeneath the startled mother's arm,

And so was still: what time we sawA foot hang down the fireplace! Then,With painful scrambling, scratched and raw,Two hands that seemed like hands of men,

Eased down two legs and a body throughThe blazing fire, and forth there cameBefore our wide and wondering viewA figure shrinking half with shame,

And half with weakness. "Sir," I said,—But with a mien of dignityThe seedy stranger raised his head:"My friends, I'm Santa Claus," said he.

But oh, how changed! That rotund faceThe new moon rivall'd, pale and thin;Where once was cheek, now empty space;Whate'er stood out, did now stand in.

His piteous legs scarce propped him up;His arms mere sickles seemed to be:But most o'erflowed our sorrow's cupWhen that we saw—or did not see—

His belly: we remembered howIt shook like a bowl of jelly fine:An earthquake could not shake it now;He had no belly—not a sign.

"Yes, yes, old friends, you well may stare:I have seen better days," he said:"But now with shrinkage, loss, and care,Your Santa Claus scarce owns his head.

"We've had such hard, hard times this yearFor goblins! Never knew the like.All Elfland's mortgaged! And we fearThat gnomes are just about to strike.

"I once was rich, and round, and hale,The whole world called me jolly brick;But listen to a piteous tale,Young Harry,—Santa Claus is sick!

"'Twas thus: a smooth-tongued railroad manComes to my house and talks to me:'I've got,' says he, 'a little planThat suits this nineteenth century.

"'Instead of driving as you do,Six reindeer slow from house to house,Let's build a Grand Trunk Railway throughFrom here to earth's last terminus.

"'We'll touch at every chimney-topAn Elevated Track, of course,Then, as we whisk you by, you'll dropEach package down: just think the force

"'You'll save, the time! Besides, we'll makeOur millions: look you, soon we willCompete for freight—and then we'll takeDame Fortune's bales of good and ill—

"'Why, she's the biggest shipper, sir,That e'er did business in this world!Then Death, that ceaseless traveller,Shall on his rounds by us be whirled.

"'When ghosts return to walk with men,We'll bring 'em cheap by steam, and fast:We'll run a branch to heaven! and thenWe'll riot, man; for then, at last,

"'We'll make with heaven a contract fairTo call each hour, from town to town,And carry the dead folks' souls up there,And bring the unborn babies down!'

"The plan seemed fair: I gave him cash,Nay every penny I could raise.My wife e'er cried, ''Tis rash, 'tis rash:'How could I know the stock-thief's ways?

"But soon I learned full well, poor fool!My woes began that wretched day.The President plied me like a tool,In lawyer's fees, and rights of way,

"Injunctions, leases, charters, IWas meshed as in a mighty maze;The stock ran low, the talk ran high,Then quickly flamed the final blaze.

"With never an inch of track—'tis true!The debts were large ... the oft-told tale.The President rolled in splendor new,—He bought my silver at the sale.

"Yes, sold me out: we've moved away.I've had to give up everything;My reindeer, even, whom I ... pray,Excuse me" ... here, o'er-sorrowing,

Poor Santa Claus burst into tears,Then calmed again: "My reindeer fleet,I gave them up: on foot, my dears,I now must plod through snow and sleet.

"Retrenchment rules in Elfland, now;Yes, every luxury is cut off,—Which, by the way, reminds me howI caught this dreadful hacking cough:

"I cut off the tail of my Ulster furredTo make young Kris a coat of stateThat very night the storm occurred!Thus we become the sport of Fate.

"For I was out till after one,Surveying chimney-tops and roofs,And planning how it could be doneWithout any reindeers' bouncing hoofs.

"'My dear,' says Mrs. Claus, that night,A most superior woman she!'It never, never can be rightThat you, deep sunk in poverty,

"This year should leave your poor old bed,And trot about, bent down with toys;There's Kris a-crying now for bread—To give to other people's boys!

"'Since you've been out, the news arrivesThe Elfs' Insurance Company's gone.Ah, Claus, those premiums! Now, our livesDepend on yours: thus griefs go on.

"And even while you're thus harassed,I do believe, if out you went,You'd go, in spite of all that's passed,To the children of that President!'

"Oh, Charley, Harry, Nimblewits,These eyes that night ne'er slept a wink;My path seemed honeycombed with pits,Naught could I do but think and think.

"But, with the day, my courage rose.Ne'er shall my boys, my boys, I cried,When Christmas morns their eyes unclose,Find empty stockings gaping wide!

"Then hewed, and whacked, and whittled I;The wife, the girls, and Kris took fire;They spun, sewed, cut,—till by and byWe made, at home, my pack entire!"

He handed me a bundle here."Now, hoist me up: there, gently: quick!Dear boys, don't look for much this year:Remember, Santa Claus is sick!"

Sidney Lanier.

OLD CHRISTMAS.

Now he who knows Old Christmas,He knows a wight of worth,For he's as good a fellowAs any on the earth;He comes warm-cloaked and coated,And buttoned to the chin;And ere he is a-nigh the door,We ope to let him in.

He comes with voice most cordial,It does one good to hear;For all the little childrenHe asks each passing year:His heart is warm and gladsome,Not like your griping elves,Who, with their wealth in plenty,Think only of themselves.

He tells us witty stories,He sings with might and main;We ne'er forget his visitTill he comes back again.With laurel green and hollyWe make the house look gay;We know that it will please him,It was his ancient way.

Oh, he's a rare old fellow;What gifts he gives away!There's not a lord in EnglandCould equal him to-day!Good luck unto Old Christmas,Long life now let us sing;He is more kind unto the poorThan any crownéd king.

Mary Howitt.

MRS. SANTA CLAUS.

The moon was like a frosted cake,The stars like flashing beadsThat round a brimming punch-bowl break'Mid spice and almond seeds;And here and there a silver beamMade bright some curling cloudUprising like the wassail's stream,Blown off by laughter loud.

It was the night of Christmas Eve,And good old Santa ClausHis door was just about to leave,When something made him pause:"I haven't kissed my wife," quoth he,"I haven't said good-by."So back he went and lovinglyHe kissed her cap awry.

Now Mrs. Claus is just a bit—The least bit—of a shrew.What wonder? Only think of it—She has so much to do.Imagine all the stocking-legs,Of every size and shape,That hang upon their Christmas pegsWith greedy mouths agape.

These she must fill, and when you seeThe northern skies aflameWith quivering light, 'tis only she—This very quaint old dame—Striking a match against the PoleHer whale-oil lamp to light,That she may see to work, poor soul,At making toys all night.

"Odd he should kiss me," this she saidBefore the sleigh had gone;"'Tis many a year since we were wed;I'll follow him anon.For faithless husbands, one and all,Ere on their loves they wait,Their wives' suspicion to forestallSeem most affectionate."

So, pulling on her seal-skin sacque,Into her husband's sleighShe slipped, and hid behind his packJust as he drove away."Great Bears!" growled Santa in his beard,"A goodly freight have I;Were't fouler weather, I had fearedThe glacier path to try."

Yet none the less they safely spedAcross the realms of snow—The glittering planets overhead,The sparkling frost below—Until the reindeer stopped beforeA mansion tall and fair,Up to whose wide and lofty doorInclined a marble stair.

So soundly all its inmates slept,They heard no stroke of hoof;No fall of foot as Santa leaptFrom pavement unto roof.So, down the chimney like a sweepHe crept, and after himWent Mrs. Claus to have a peepAt chambers warm and dim.

As luck would have it, there was hungA stocking by the fireTo wear which no one over-youngCould fittingly aspire:Long, slender, graceful—it was justThe thing to fill the heartOf Mrs. C. with deep distrust;And—well—it played its part.

Scowling, she watched her husband fillThe silken foot and legWith bonbons, fruit, and toys untilIt almost broke its peg. "My!" whispered Santa, "here's a crop.This little boy is wise;He knows I fill 'em to the top,No matter what the size."

But Mrs. Claus misunderstood,Like every jealous wife;She *would* make bad things out of good,To feed her inward strife.Snapped she unto herself: "The minxSha'n't have a single thing!I'll take 'em home again, methinks,Nor leave a stick or string!"

So said, so done; and all that nightShe followed Santa's wake,And as he stuffed the stockings tight,She every one did take,Stowing them all unseen away,In order grimly neat,Within the dark box of the sleigh,All underneath the seat.

And when gray dawn broke, and allThe bells began to peal,And tiny forms down many a hallAnd stairway 'gan to steal,[Pg 162]In vain each chimney-piece they sought—Those weeping girls and boys—For Christmas morn had come and broughtNo candy and no toys.

Charles Henry Lüders.

SANTA CLAUS TO LITTLE ETHEL.

(IN ANSWER TO HER LETTER, GIVING HIM A LIST OF HER CHRISTMAS WANTS.)

My dear little Ethel,I fear that the breath'llBe out of our bodies before we get through;Day in and day outWe are rushing about,And you haven't a notion how much there's to do.

Ever since last December,When you may rememberI paid you a visit at dear Elsinore,There's not been a minuteWith a resting-place in it,And my nose has not once been outside of the door.

My shop has been going,My bellows a-blowing,My hammers and tongs and a thousand odd tools,Never give up the battle,But click, bang, and rattleLike ten million children in ten thousand schools.

Dear me, but I'm weary!And yet, my small deary,I read all the letters as fast as they come;If I didn't,—good gracious!The house is not spacious,And the letters would soon squeeze me out of my home.

"I would like a nice sled,And a dolly's soft bed,With a night-gown and bed-clothes of pretty bright stuffs,And paints, and a caseWhere my books I may place,And besides all these things, Dolly's collars and cuffs."

That's a pretty big list!But may I be kissedOn the back of my head by a crazy mule's hoof,If the list I don't fill,Though it takes all the skillOf every stout workman beneath my broad roof.

"Hans, Yakob, and Karl!Let me not hear a snarl, Or a growl, or a grumble come out of your heads;To work now, instanter!Trot, gallop, and canter,And finish this job ere you go to your beds!"

So I set them to workWith a jump and a jerk,And everything's finished in beautiful style.Christmas Eve's here again,And I'm off with my train,Every reindeer prepared for ten seconds a mile.

I shall slip down the flueWith this letter for you,So softly, for fear I your slumbers might break.Not a word will I speak,But I'll kiss your soft cheek,And be gone in a jiffy, before you awake.

Should you find I've forgotAny part of the lotThat I ordered prepared and all marked with your name,Let me just add a word,So if that has occurred,You will know just exactly how I was to blame.

The fact is, my dear,As I go, year by year,[Pg 166]Up and down these straight chimneys, while you are in bed,The bumps and the scratchesThat Santa Claus catchesHave rubbed all the hair from the top of his head.

And my brain being bareOf my cover of hair,Is rapidly losing its power, my pet!Sometimes, after all's fixed,I get everything mixed,And you must forgive if I ever forget.

Good-by, Ethel dear!May the coming New YearBring all kinds of blessings to you from above;Make you happier and better:And so my long letterMust close, with a great deal of Santa Claus's love.

Francis Wells.

The Season's Reveries.

"How many times have you sat at gazeTill the mouldering fire forgot to blaze,Shaping among the whimsical coalsFancies and figures and shining goals!"

Lowell.

GUESTS AT YULE.

*Noel! Noel!*Thus sounds each Christmas bellAcross the winter snow.But what are the little footprints allThat mark the path from the churchyard wall?They are those of the children waked to-nightFrom sleep by the Christmas bells and light:Ring sweetly, chimes! Soft, soft, my rhymes!Their beds are under the snow.

*Noel! Noel!*Carols each Christmas bell.What are the wraiths of mistThat gather anear the window-paneWhere the winter frost all day has lain?They are soulless elves, who fain would peerWithin and laugh at our Christmas cheer:Ring fleetly, chimes! Swift, swift, my rhymes!They are made of the mocking mist.

*Noel! Noel!*Cease, cease, each Christmas bell!Under the holly bough,Where the happy children throng and shout,What shadow seems to flit about?Is it the mother, then, who diedEre the greens were sere last Christmas-tide?Hush, falling chimes! Cease, cease, my rhymes!The guests are gathered now.

Edmund Clarence Stedman.

CHRISTMAS IN INDIA.

Dim dawn the tamarisks—the sky is saffron-yellow—As the women in the village grind the corn,And the parrots seek the riverside, each calling to his fellowThat the day, the staring eastern day, is born.Oh, the white dust on the highway! Oh, the stenches in the by-way!Oh, the clammy fog that hovers over earth!And at home they're making merry 'neath the white and scarlet berry—What part have India's exiles in their mirth?

Full day behind the tamarisks—the sky is blue and staring—As the cattle crawl afield beneath the yoke,And they bear one o'er the field-path who is past all hope or caring,To the ghat below the curling wreaths of smoke.Call on Rama, going slowly, as ye bear a brother lowly—Call on Rama—he may hear, perhaps, your voice! With our hymn-books and our psalters we appeal to other altars,And to-day we bid "good Christian men rejoice!"

High noon above the tamarisks—the sun is hot above us—As at home the Christmas Day is breaking wan,They will drink our healths at dinner—those who tell us how they love us,And forget us till another year be gone!Oh, the toil that knows no breaking! Oh! the heimweh, ceaseless, aching!Oh, the black, dividing sea and alien plain!Youth was cheap—wherefore we sold it. Gold was good—we hoped to hold it,And to-day we know the fulness of our gain.

Gray dusk behind the tamarisks—the parrots fly together—As the sun is sinking slowly over home;And his last ray seems to mock us, shackled in a lifelong tetherThat drags us back, howe'er so far we roam.Hard her service, poor her payment—she in ancient, tattered raiment—India, she the grim stepmother of our kind.If a year of life be lent her, if her temple's shrine we enter,The door is shut—we may not look behind.

Black night behind the tamarisks—the owls begin their chorus—As the conches from the temple scream and bray.With the fruitless years behind us and the hopeless years before us,Let us honor, O, my brothers, Christmas Day!Call a truce, then, to our labors—let us feast with friends and neighbors,And be merry as the custom of our caste;For, if "faint and forced the laughter," and if sadness follow after,We are richer by one mocking Christmas past.

Rudyard Kipling.

CHRISTMAS VIOLETS.

Last night I found the violetsYou sent me once across the sea;From gardens that the winter frets,In summer lands they came to me.

Still fragrant of the English earth,Still humid from the frozen dew,To me they spoke of Christmas mirth,They spoke of England, spoke of you.

The flowers are scentless, black, and sere,The perfume long has passed away;The sea whose tides are year by yearIs set between us, chill and gray.

But you have reached a windless age,The haven of a happy clime;You do not dread the winter's rage,Although we missed the summer-time.

And like the flower's breath over sea,Across the gulf of time and pain,To-night returns the memoryOf love that lived not all in vain.

Andrew Lang.

The Season's Reveries

DICKENS RETURNS ON CHRISTMAS DAY.

(A ragged girl in Drury Lane was heard to exclaim, "Dickens dead? Then will Father Christmas die, too?" June 9, 1870.)

"Dickens is dead!" Beneath that grievous cry London seemed shivering in the summer heat; Strangers took up the tale like friends that meet: "Dickens is dead!" said they, and hurried by; Street children stopped their games—they knew not why, But some new night seemed darkening down the street; A girl in rags, staying her way-worn feet, Cried, "Dickens dead? Will Father Christmas die?"

City he loved, take courage on thy way! He loves thee still in all thy joys and fears: Though he whose smiles made bright thine eyes of gray—Whose brave sweet voice, uttering thy tongueless years, Made laughters bubble through thy sea of tears—Is gone, Dickens returns on Christmas Day!

Theodore Watts.

A GRIEF AT CHRISTMAS.

FROM "IN MEMORIAM."

First Year.

The time draws near the birth of ChristThe moon is hid; the night is still;The Christmas bells from hill to hillAnswer each other in the mist.

Four voices of four hamlets round,From far and near, on mead and moor,Swell out and fail, as if a doorWere shut between me and the sound:

Each voice four changes on the wind,That now dilate, and now decrease,Peace and good-will, good-will and peace,Peace and good-will, to all mankind.

This year I slept and woke with pain,I almost wish'd no more to wake,And that my hold on life would breakBefore I heard those bells again:

But they my troubled spirit rule,For they controll'd me when a boy;They bring me sorrow touched with joy,The merry merry bells of Yule.

With such compelling cause to grieveAs daily vexes household peace,And chains regret to his decease,How dare we keep our Christmas-eve;

Which brings no more a welcome guestTo enrich the threshold of our nightWith shower'd largess of delight,In dance and song and game and jest.

Yet go, and while the holly boughsEntwine the cold baptismal font,Make one wreath more for Use and Wont,That guard the portals of the house;

Old sisters of a day gone by,Gray nurses, loving nothing new;Why should they miss their yearly dueBefore their time? They too will die.

With trembling fingers did we weaveThe holly round the Christmas hearth;A rainy cloud possess'd the earth,And sadly fell our Christmas-eve.

At our old pastimes in the hallWe gambol'd, making vain pretenceOf gladness, with an awful senseOf one mute Shadow watching all.

We paused: the winds were in the beech:We heard them sweep the winter land;And in a circle hand-in-handSat silent, looking each at each.

Then echo-like our voices rang;We sung, tho' every eye was dim,A merry song we sang with himLast year: impetuously we sang:

We ceased: a gentler feeling creptUpon us: surely rest is meet."They rest," we said, "their sleep is sweet,"And silence follow'd, and we wept.

Our voices took a higher range;Once more we sang: "They do not dieNor lose their mortal sympathy,Nor change to us, although they change;

"Rapt from the fickle and the frailWith gather'd power, yet the samePierces the keen seraphic flameFrom orb to orb, from veil to veil."

Rise, happy morn, rise, holy morn,Draw forth the cheerful day from night:O Father, touch the east, and lightThe light that shone when Hope was born.

Second Year.

Again at Christmas did we weaveThe holly round the Christmas hearth;The silent snow possessed the earth,And calmly fell on Christmas-eve:

The yule-clog sparkled keen with frost,No wing of wind the region swept,But over all things brooding sleptThe quiet sense of something lost.

As in the winters left behind,Again our ancient games had place,The mimic picture's breathing grace,And dance and song and hoodman-blind.

Who show'd a token of distress?No single tear, no mark of pain:O sorrow, then can sorrow wane?O grief, can grief be changed to less?

O last regret, regret can die!No—mixt with all this mystic frame,Her deep relations are the same,But with long use her tears are dry.

Third Year.

The time draws near the birth of Christ;The moon is hid, the night is still;A single church below the hillIs pealing, folded in the mist.

A single peal of bells below,That wakens at this hour of restA single murmur in the breast,That these are not the bells I know.

Like strangers' voices here they sound,In lands where not a memory strays,Nor landmark breathes of other days,But all is new unhallow'd ground.

To-night ungather'd let us leaveThis laurel, let this holly stand:We live within the stranger's land,And strangely falls our Christmas-eve.

Our father's dust is left aloneAnd silent under other snows:There in due time the woodbine blows,The violet comes, but we are gone.

No more shall wayward grief abuseThe genial hour with mask and mime;For change of place, like growth of time,Has broke the bond of dying use.

Let cares that petty shadows cast,By which our lives are chiefly proved,A little spare the night I loved,And hold it solemn to the past.

But let no footsteps beat the floor,Nor bowl of wassail mantle warm;For who would keep an ancient formThro' which the spirit breathes no more?

Be neither song, nor game, nor feast;Nor harp be touch'd, nor flute be blown;No dance, no motion, save aloneWhat lightens in the lucid east

Of rising worlds by yonder wood.Long sleeps the summer in the seed;Run out your measured arcs, and leadThe closing cycle rich in good.

Ring out wild bells, to the wild sky,The flying cloud, the frosty light:The year is dying in the night:Ring out, wild bells, and let him die.

Ring out the old, ring in the new,Ring, happy bells, across the snow;The year is going, let him go;Ring out the false, ring in the true.

Ring out the grief that saps the mind,For those that here we see no more;Ring out the feud of rich and poor;Ring in redress of all mankind.

Ring out the slowly dying cause,And ancient forms of party strife;Ring in the nobler modes of life,With sweeter manners, purer laws.

Ring out the want, the care, the sin,The faithless coldness of the times;Ring out, ring out, my mournful rhymes,But ring the fuller minstrel in:

Ring out false pride in place and blood, The civic slander and the spite; Ring in the love of truth and right, Ring in the common love of good.

Ring out old shapes of foul disease; Ring out the narrowing lust of gold; Ring out the thousand wars of old, Ring in the thousand years of peace.

Ring in the valiant man and free, The larger heart, the kindlier hand; Ring out the darkness of the land, Ring in the Christ that is to be.

Lord Tennyson.

MY SISTER'S SLEEP.

She fell asleep on Christmas-eve:At length the long-ungranted shadeOf weary eyelids overweigh'dThe pain naught else might yet relieve.

Our mother, who had leaned all dayOver the bed from chime to chime,Then raised herself for the first time,And as she sat her down did pray.

Her little work-table was spreadWith work to finish. For the glareMade by her candle, she had careTo work some distance from the bed.

Without there was a cold moon up,Of winter radiance sheer and thin;The hollow halo it was inWas like an icy crystal cup.

Through the small room, with subtle soundOf flame, by vents the fireshine droveAnd reddened. In its dim alcoveThe mirror shed a clearness round.

I had been sitting up some nights,And my tired mind felt weak and blank;Like a sharp, strengthening wine it drankThe stillness and the broken lights.

Twelve struck. That sound, by dwindling yearsHeard in each hour, crept off; and thenThe ruffled silence spread again,Like water that a pebble stirs.

Our mother rose from where she sat:Her needles, as she laid them down,Met lightly, and her silken gownSettled: no other noise than that.

"Glory unto the Newly Born,"So as said angels, she did say;Because we were in Christmas-day,Though it would still be long till morn.

Just then in the room over usThere was a pushing back of chairs,As some one had sat unawaresSo late, now heard the hour, and rose.

With anxious, softly-stepping hasteOur mother went where Margaret lay,Fearing the sounds o'erhead—should theyHave broken her long-watched-for rest!

She stooped an instant, calm, and turned;But suddenly turned back again;And all her features seemed in painWith woe, and her eyes gazed and yearned.

For my part, I but hid my face,And held my breath, and spoke no word;There was none spoken; but I heardThe silence for a little space.

Our mother bowed herself and wept;And both my arms fell, and I said,"God knows I knew that she was dead,"And there, all white, my sister slept.

Then kneeling upon Christmas mornA little after twelve o'clock,We said, ere the first quarter struck,"Christ's blessing on the newly born!"

Dante Gabriel Rossetti.

CHRISTMAS IN EDINBOROUGH.

I.

Sheath'd is the river as it glideth by,Frost-pearl'd are all the boughs of forests old,The sheep are huddling close upon the wold,And over them the stars tremble on high.Pure joys these winter nights around me lie;'Tis fine to loiter through the lighted streetsAt Christmas-time, and guess from brow and paceThe doom and history of each one we meet,What kind of heart beats in each dusky case;Whiles, startled by the beauty of a faceIn a shop-light a moment. Or instead,To dream of silent fields where calm and deepThe sunshine lieth like a golden sleep—Recalling sweetest looks of summers dead.

Alexander Smith.

CHRISTMAS IN EDINBOROUGH.

II.

Joy like a stream flows through the Christmas streets,But I am sitting in my silent room,Sitting all silent in congenial gloomTo-night, while half the world the other greetsWith smiles and grasping hands and drinks and meats,I sit and muse on my poetic doom;Like the dim scent within a budded rose,A joy is folded in my heart; and whenI think on poets nurtured 'mong the throesAnd by the lowly hearths of common men,—Think of their works, some song, some swelling odeWith gorgeous music growing to a close,Deep muffled as the dead-march of a god,—My heart is burning to be one of those.

Alexander Smith.

AROUND THE CHRISTMAS LAMP.

The wind may shout as it likes without;It may rage, but cannot harm us;For a merrier din shall resound within,And our Christmas cheer will warm us.There is gladness to all at its ancient call,While its ruddy fires are gleaming,And from far and near, o'er the landscape drear,The Christmas light is streaming.

All the frozen ground is in fetters bound;Ho! the yule-log we will burn it;For Christmas is come in ev'ry home,To summer our hearts will turn it.There is gladness to all at its ancient call,While its ruddy fires are gleaming;And from far and near, o'er the landscape drear,The Christmas light is streaming.

J. L. Molloy.

CHRISTMAS-EVE.

Alone—with one fair star for company,The loveliest star among the hosts of night,While the gray tide ebbs with the ebbing light—I pace along the darkening wintry sea.Now round the yule-log and the glittering treeTwinkling with festive tapers, eyes as brightSparkle with Christmas joys and young delightAs each one gathers to his family.

But I—a waif on earth where'er I roam—Uprooted with life's bleeding hopes and fears,From that one heart that was my heart's sole home,Feel the old pang pierce through the severing years,And as I think upon the years to come,That fair star trembles through my falling tears.

Mathilde Blind.

WONDERLAND.

Lo! I will make my homeIn the beautiful Land of Books;Where the friends of childhood roamThrough most delightful nooks.

I'll rent the unfinished floorIn Aladdin's palace built,Whose walls, to the outer door,Are ivory and gilt.

And the Caliph— Haroun—thereWill pass in his deft disguise;But him I'll know by his airSo grand, and his eagle eyes.

And Cinderella, too,Will weep when her sisters whip her:And I'll be the Prince—or you—Who will find her crystal slipper.

And O, what fun it will beWith Robin the Bobbin to feast,Or to frequently call and seeThe Beauty and the Beast.

For she and you and IAnd the Rusty Dusty MillerWill eat of a Christmas-PieWith Jack the Giant-Killer.

Then come, let us make our homesIn the most frequented nooksOf the land of elves and gnomes,In the beautiful Land of Books!

Charles Henry Lüders.

WAITING.

As little children in a darkened hallAt Christmas-tide await the opening door,Eager to tread the fairy-haunted floorAround the tree with goodly gifts for all,Oft in the darkness to each other call,— Trying to guess their happiness before—Or knowing elders eagerly imploreTo tell what fortune unto them may fall,—

So wait we in time's dim and narrow room,And, with strange fancies or another's thought,Try to divine before the curtain riseThe wondrous scene; forgetting that the gloomMust shortly flee from what the ages sought,—The Father's long-planned gift of Paradise.

C. H. Crandall.

AUNT MARY.

A CORNISH CHRISTMAS CHANT.

Now of all the trees by the king's highway,Which do you love the best?O! the one that is green upon Christmas-day,The bush with the bleeding breast.Now the holly with her drops of blood for me:For that is our dear Aunt Mary's tree.

Its leaves are sweet with our Saviour's name,'Tis a plant that loves the poor:Summer and winter it shines the sameBeside the cottage door.O! the holly with her drops of blood for me:For that is our kind Aunt Mary's tree.

'Tis a bush that the birds will never leave:They sing in it all day long;But sweetest of all upon Christmas-eveIs to hear the robin's song.'Tis the merriest sound upon earth and sea:For it comes from our own Aunt Mary's tree.

So, of all that grow by the king's highway,I love that tree the best;'Tis a bower for the birds upon Christmas-day,The bush of the bleeding breast.O! the holly with her drops of blood for me:For that is our sweet Aunt Mary's tree.

Robert Stephen Hawker.

THE GLAD NEW DAY.

And why should not that land rejoice,And darkness flee away,When on its dim, benighted hillsHas dawned the glad new day?For now behold the shepherds go,The wondrous babe to see;Ah, then methinks that all aroundWas one grand jubilee!

Rejoice, ye nations blest with peace,Let all the earth be glad;The Prince of Peace comes down to-day,In robes of pity clad.Yea, thus should all mankind rejoiceOn this glad day of love;But yet, alas! how far we areFrom those blest heights above!

Ah! for the time when men shall spendThis day as all men should,When angels shall with joy attend,And dwell among the good.Then will this earth an Eden be,A Paradise of love;And all shall know the perfect blissOf those bright realms above.

Thomas Moore.

UNDER THE HOLLY BOUGH.

Ye who have scorned each otherIn this fast fading year,Or wronged a friend or brother,Come gather humbly here:Let sinned against and sinningForget their strife's beginning,Be links no longer brokenBeneath the holly bough,Be sweet forgiveness spokenBeneath the holly bough.

Ye who have loved each otherIn this fast fading year,Sister, or friend, or brother,Come gather happy here:And let your hearts grow fonderAs mem'ry glad shall ponderOld loves and later wooingBeneath the holly bough,So sweet in their renewingBeneath the holly bough.

Ye who have nourished sadnessIn this fast fading year,Estranged from joy and gladness,Come gather hopeful here No more let useless sorrowPursue you night and morrow;Come join in our embracesBeneath the holly bough;Take heart, uncloud your facesBeneath the holly bough.

Charles Mackay.

THE DAWN OF CHRISTMAS.

A cold it is and middle night: The moon looks down the snow, As if an angel, clad in white, Carried her lanthorn so That, going forth the streets of light, She made an earthward glow.

A drift enfolds the chapel eaves Like downy coverlet; And, garnered into whited sheaves, The graves are harvest-set Waiting the yeoman. All the panes Are rich with rimy fret.

The sexton mounts the outer stair Where chilly sparrows cower— And bells ring down the winter air From forth the snowy tower; For, muffled deep in drift, the clock Hath struck the Christmas hour.

And over barn, and buried stack, And out the naked copse, And where the owl sits plump and black Amid the chestnut tops The branches echo back the bells, Like dulcet organ stops.

For blast of wind and creak of bough And rustle of the frost, And winter's inner voice—avow The holy hour is crossed, And far, mysterious music sounds, Sweet like a harping host.

H. S. M.

BALLADE OF CHRISTMAS GHOSTS.

Between the moonlight and the fire,In winter evenings long ago,What ghosts I raised at your desire,To make your leaping blood run slow!How old, how grave, how wise we grow!What Christmas ghost can make us chill—Save these that troop in mournful row,The ghosts we all can raise at will?

The beasts can talk in barn and byreOn Christmas-eve, old legends know.As one by one the years retire,We men fall silent then, I trow—Such sights has memory to show,Such voices from the distance thrill.Ah me! they come with Christmas snow,The ghosts we all can raise at will.

Oh, children of the village choir,Your carols on the midnight throw!Oh, bright across the mist and mire,Ye ruddy hearths of Christmas glow!Beat back the shades, beat down the woe,Renew the strength of mortal will; Be welcome, all, to come or go,The ghosts we all can raise at will.

Friend, *sursum corda,* soon or slowWe part, like guests who've joyed their fill;Forget them not, nor mourn them so,The ghosts we all can raise at will!

Andrew Lang.

THE VILLAGE CHRISTMAS.

Meantime the village rouses up the fire:While well attested, and as well believed,Heard solemn, goes the goblin story round,Till superstitious horror creeps o'er all.Or, frequent in the sounding hall, they wakeThe rural gambol. Rustic mirth goes round;The simple joke that takes the shepherd's heart,Easily pleased; the long, loud laugh, sincere;The kiss, snatched hasty from the side-long maid,On purpose guardless, or pretending sleep;The leap, the slap, the haul; and, shook to notesOf native music, the respondent dance,Thus jocund fleets with them the winter-night.

James Thomson.

WINTER.

A wrinkled, crabbéd man they picture thee,Old winter, with a rugged beard as grayAs the long moss upon the apple-tree;Blue-lipt, an ice-drop at thy sharp blue nose,Close muffled up, and on thy dreary wayPlodding alone through sleet and drifting snows.They should have drawn thee by the high-heapt hearth,Old winter! seated in thy great armed-chair,Watching the children at their Christmas mirth;Or circled by them as thy lips declareSome merry jest, or tale of murder dire,Or troubled spirit that disturbs the night;Pausing at times to rouse the smouldering fire,Or taste the old October brown and bright.

Robert Southey.

DECEMBER.

And after him came next the chill December: Yet he, through merry feasting which he made, And great bonfires, did not the cold remember; His Saviour's birth his mind so much did glad: Upon a shaggy-bearded goat he rode, The same wherewith Dan Jove in tender years, They say, was nourisht by th' Idæan Mayd; And in his hand a broad deep bowle he beares, Of which he freely drinks an health to all his peeres.

Edmund Spenser.

CHRISTMAS WEATHER IN SCOTLAND.

A winter day! the feather-silent snowThickens the air with strange delight, and laysA fairy carpet on the barren lea.No sun, yet all around that inward lightWhich is in purity,—a soft moonshine,The silvery dimness of a happy dream.How beautiful! afar on moorland ways,Bosomed by mountains, darkened by huge glens,(Where the lone altar raised by Druid handsStands like a mournful phantom,) hidden cloudsLet fall soft beauty, till each green fir branchIs plumed and tasselled, till each heather stalkIs delicately fringed. The sycamores,Through all their mystical entanglementOf boughs, are draped with silver. All the greenOf sweet leaves playing with the subtle airIn dainty murmuring; the obstinate droneOf limber bees that in the monk's-hood bellsHouse diligent; the imperishable glowOf summer sunshine never more confessedThe harmony of nature, the divine,Diffusive spirit of the beautiful.Out in the snowy dimness, half revealedLike ghosts in glimpsing moonshine, wildly runThe children in bewildering delight.There is a living glory in the air,—A glory in the hushed air, in the soulA palpitating wonder hushed in awe.

Softly—with delicate softness—as the lightQuickens in the undawned east; and silently—With definite silence—as the stealing dawnDapples the floating clouds, slow fall, slow fall,With indecisive motion eddying down,The white-winged flakes,—calm as the sleep of sound,Dim as a dream. The silver-misted airShines with mild radiance, as when through a cloudOf semilucent vapor shines the moon.I saw last evening (when the ruddy sun,Enlarged and strange, sank low and visibly,Spreading fierce orange o'er the west) a sceneOf winter in his milder mood. Green fields,Which no kine cropped, lay damp; and naked treesThrew skeleton shadows. Hedges, thickly grown,Twined into compact firmness, with no leaves,Trembled in jewelled fretwork as the sunTo lustre touched the tremulous water-drops.Alone, nor whistling as his fellows doIn fabling poem and provincial song, The ploughboy shouted to his reeking train;And at the clamor, from a neighboring fieldArose, with whirr of wings, a flock of rooksMore clamorous; and through the frosted air,Blown wildly here and there without a law,They flew, low-grumbling out loquacious croaks.Red sunset brightened all things; streams ran redYet coldly; and before the unwholesome east,Searching the bones and breathing ice, blew downThe hill, with a dry whistle, by the fireIn chamber twilight rested I at home.

But now what revelation of fair change,O Giver of the seasons and the days!Creator of all elements, pale mists,Invisible great winds and exact frost!How shall I speak the wonder of thy snow?What though we know its essence and its birth,Can quick expound, in philosophic wise,The how, and whence, and manner of its fall;Yet, oh, the inner beauty and the life—The life that is in snow! The virgin-softAnd utter purity of the down-flake,Falling upon its fellow with no sound!Unblown by vulgar winds, innumerous flakesFall gently, with the gentleness of love!The earth is cherished, for beneath the soft,Pure uniformity is gently born Warmth and rich mildness, fitting the dead rootsFor the resuscitation of the spring.Now while I write, the wonder clothes the vale,Calmed every wind and loaded every grove;And looking through the implicated boughsI see a gleaming radiance.

Sparkling snow, Refined by morning-footed frost so still, Mantles each bough; and such a windless hushBreathes through the air, it seems the fairy glenAbout some phantom palace, pale abodeOf fabled Sleeping Beauty. Songless birdsFlit restlessly about the breathless wood, Waiting the sudden breaking of the charm; And as they quickly spring on nimble wingFrom the white twig, a sparkling shower fallsStarlike. It is not whiteness, but a clearOutshining of all purity, which takesThe winking eyes with such a silvery gleam. No sunshine, and the sky is all one cloud. The vale seems lonely, ghostlike; while aloudThe housewife's voice is heard with doubled sound. I have not words to speak the perfect show; The ravishment of beauty; the delightOf silent purity; the sanctityOf inspiration which o'erflows the

So thus with fair delapsion softly fallsThe sacred shower; and when the shortened dayDejected dies in the low streaky west, The rising moon displays a cold blue night, And keen as steel the east wind sprinkles ice. Thicker than bees, about the waxing moonGather the punctual stars. Huge whitened hillsRise glimmering to the blue verge of the night, Ghostlike, and striped with narrow glens of firsBlack-waving, solemn. O'er the Luggie-streamGathers a veiny film of ice, and creepsWith elfin feet around each stone and reed, Working fine masonry; while o'er the dam, Dashing, a noise of waters fills the clearAnd nitrous air. All the dark, wintry hoursSharply the winds from the white level moorsKeen whistle. Timorous in his homely bedThe school-boy listens, fearful lest gaunt wolvesOr beasts, whose uncouth forms in ancient booksHe has beheld, at creaking shutters pullHowling. And when at last the languid dawnIn wind redness re-illumines the eastWith ineffectual fire, an intense blueSeverely vivid o'er the snowy hillsGleams chill, while hazy, half-transparent cloudsSlow-range the freezing ether of the west.Along the woods the keenly vehement blastsWail, and disrobe the mantled boughs, and flingA snow-dust everywhere. Thus wears the day: While grandfather over the well-watched fireHangs cowering, with a cold drop at his nose.

Now underneath the ice the Luggie growls,And to the polished smoothness curlers comeRudely ambitious. Then for happy hoursThe clinking stones are slid from wary hands,And Barleycorn, best wine for surly airs,Bites i' th' mouth, and ancient jokes are cracked.And oh, the journey homeward, when the sun,Low-rounding to the west, in ruddy glowSinks large, and all the amber-skirted clouds,His flaming retinue, with dark'ning glowDiverge! The broom is brandished as the signOf conquest, and impetuously they boastOf how this shot was played,—with what a bendPeculiar—the perfection of all art—That stone came rolling grandly to the TeeWith victory crowned, and flinging wide the restIn lordly crash! Within the village innThey by the roaring chimney sit, and quaffThe beaded Usqueba with sugar dashed.O, when the precious liquid fires the brainTo joy, and every heart beats fast with mirthAnd ancient fellowship, what nervy graspsOf horny hands o'er tables of rough oak! What singing of Lang Syne till tear-drops shine,And friendships brighten as the evening wanes!

David Gray.

SIR GALAHAD.

When on my goodly charger borneThro' dreaming towns I go,The cock crows ere the Christmas morn,The streets are dumb with snow.The tempest crackles on the leadsAnd, ringing, springs from brand and mail;But o'er the dark a glory spreads,And gilds the driving hail.

Lord Tennyson.

"Too Happy, Happy Tree"

A THOUGHT FOR THE TIME.

In a drear-nighted December,Too happy, happy tree,Thy branches ne'er rememberTheir green felicity:The north cannot undo themWith a sleety whistle through them;Nor frozen thawings glue themFrom budding at the prime.

In a drear-nighted December,Too happy, happy brook,Thy bubblings ne'er rememberApollo's summer look;But with a sweet forgetting,They stay their crystal fretting,Never, never pettingAbout the frozen time.

Ah! would't were so with manyA gentle girl and boy!But were there ever anyWrithed not at passèd joy?To know the change and feel it,When there is none to heal it,Nor numbèd sense to steal it,Was never said in rhyme.

John Keats.

BALLADE OF THE WINTER FIRESIDE.

An ingle-blaze and a steaming jug;A lamp and a lazy book;And, deep in a doubled, downy rugYour feet to the warmest nook.And wherever the eye may crook,A print or a tumbled tome—For the kettle sings on the blackened hook,And hey! for the sweets of home!

What though the traveller toil and tugWhere sleety drifts be shook?What though i' the churchyard graves be dug;And sweethearts be forsook?A hearth, and a careful cook,And cares may go or come!For the kettle sings on the blackened hook,And hey! for the sweets of home!

But—curtains down and an elbow hug;A maid that comes to a look;A boy to carry a rimy logFrom over the frozen brook—And, a fig for the cawing rook,Or ghosts in the ruddy gloam!For the kettle sings on the blackened hook,And hey! for the sweets of home!

Envoi.

And yet—or I be mistook—To a friend the cup should foam;For the kettle sings on the blackened hook,And hey! for the sweets of home!

H. S. M.

A CATCH BY THE HEARTH.

Sing we all merrilyChristmas is here,The day that we love bestOf days in the year.

Bring forth the holly,The box, and the bay,Deck out our cottageFor glad Christmas-day.

Sing we all merrily,Draw round the fire,Sister and brother,Grandson and sire.

SALLY IN OUR ALLEY.

When Christmas comes about again, O then I shall have money; I'll hoard it up, and box it all, I'll give it to my honey: I would it were ten thousand pound, I'd give it all to Sally; She is the darling of my heart, And she lives in our alley.

H. Carey.

LITTLE MOTHER.

A GERMAN FANCY.

Little mother, why must you go?The children play by the white bedside,The world is merry for Christmas-tide,And what would you do in the falling snow?

They sleep by now in the ember-glow,Hushed to dream in a child's delight,For wonders happen on Christmas night:Little mother, why must you go?

The flakes fall and the night grows late.Oh, slender figure and small wet feet,Where do you haste through the lamp-lit street,And out and away by the fortress gate?

It is drear and chill where the dear lie dead,Yet light enough with the snow to see;But what would you do with that Christmas-treeAt the tiny mound that is baby's bed?

A Christmas-tree with its tinsel gold!Oh, how should I not have a thought for thee,When the children sleep in their dream of glee,Poor little grave but a twelvemonth old!

Little mother, your heart is brave,You kiss the cross in the drifted snow,Kneel for a moment, rise and goAnd leave your tree by the tiny grave.

While the living slept by the warm fireside, And flakes fell white on your Christmas toy, I think that its angel wept for joy Because you remembered the one that died.

Rennell Rodd.

OCCIDENT AND ORIENT.

How will it dawn, the coming Christmas-day?A northern Christmas, such as painters love,And kinsfolk shaking hands but once a year,And dames who tell old legends by the fire?Red sun, blue sky, white snow, and pearléd ice,Keen ringing air, which sets the blood on fire,And makes the old man merry with the youngThrough the short sunshine, through the longer night?

Or southern Christmas, dark and dank with mist,And heavy with the scent of steaming leaves,And rose-buds mouldering on the dripping porch;On twilight, without rise or set of sun,Till beetles drone along the hollow laneAnd round the leafless hawthorns, flitting batsHawk the pale moths of winter? Welcome then,At best, the flying gleam, the flying shower,The rain-pools glittering on the long white roads,And shadows sweeping on from down to downBefore the salt Atlantic gale! Yet comeIn whatsoever garb, or gay or sad, Come fair, come foul, 'twill still be Christmas-day.

How will it dawn, the coming Christmas-day?To sailors lounging on the lonely deckBeneath the rushing trade-wind? or, to himWho by some noisome harbor of the eastWatches swart arms roll down the precious bales,Spoils of the tropic forests; year by yearAmid the din of heathen voices, groaning,Himself half heathen? How to those—brave hearts!Who toil with laden loins and sinking strideBeside the bitter wells of treeless sandsToward the peaks which flood the ancient Nile,To free a tyrant's captives? How to those—New patriarchs of the new-found under world—Who stand like Jacob, on the virgin lawns,And count their flocks' increase? To them that day,Shall dawn in glory, and solstitial blazeOf full midsummer sun: to them that mornGay flowers beneath their feet, gay birds aloftShall tell of naught but summer; but to them,Ere yet, unwarned by carol or by chime,They spring into the saddle, thrills may comeFrom that great heart of Christendom which beats Round all the worlds; and gracious thoughts of youth;Of steadfast folk, who worship God at home,Of wise words, learnt beside their mother's knee;Of innocent faces, upturned once againIn awe and joy to listen to the taleOf God made man, and in a manger laid:May soften, purify, and raise the soulFrom selfish cares, and growing lust of gainAnd phantoms of this dream, which some call life,Toward eternal facts; for here or thereSummer or winter, 'twill be Christmas-day.

Blest day, which aye reminds us year by yearWhat 'tis to be a man: to curb and spurnThe tyrant in us: that ignobler selfWhich boasts, not loathes, its likeness to the brute,And owns no good save ease, no ill save pain,No purpose, save its share in that wild warIn which, through countless ages, living thingsCompete in internecine greed—ah, God!Are we as creeping things, which have no Lord?That we are brutes, great God, we know too well:Apes daintier-featured; silly birds who flauntTheir plumes, unheeding of the fowler's step; Spiders who catch with paper, not with webs;Tigers who slay with cannon and sharp steel,Instead of teeth and claws; all these we are.Are we no more than these save in degree?No more than these; and born but to compete—To envy and devour, like beast or herbMere fools of nature; puppets of strong lusts, Taking the sword to perish with the swordUpon the universal battle-field, Even as the things upon the moor outside?

The heath eats up green grass and delicate flowers, The pine eats up the heath, the grub the pine, The finch the grub, the hawk the silly finch; And man, the mightiest of all beasts of prey, Eats what he lists;—the strong eat up the weak; The many eat the few; great nations, small; And he who cometh in the name of allShall, greediest, triumph by the greed of all; And armed by his own victims, eat up all. While even out of the eternal heavensLooks patient down the great magnanimous GodWho, Maker of all worlds, did sacrificeAll to himself. Nay, but himself to oneWho taught mankind on that first Christmas-day What 'twas to be a man: to give not take; To serve not rule; to nourish not devour; To help, not crush; if need, to die, not live.

Oh, blessed day which givest the eternal lieTo self and sense and all the brute within; Oh, come to us, amid this war of life, To hall and hovel, come, to all who toilIn senate, shop, or study; and to thoseWho sundered by the wastes of half a worldIll warned, and sorely tempted, ever faceNature's brute powers and men unmanned to brutes, Come to them, blest and blessing, Christmas-day. Tell them once more the tale of Bethlehem, The kneeling shepherds and the Babe Divine, And keep them men indeed, fair Christmas-day.

Charles Kingsley.

THE BLESSED DAY.

Awake, my soul, and come away:Put on thy best array;Lest if thou longer stayThou lose some minutes of so blest a day.Go runAnd bid good-morrow to the sun;Welcome his safe returnTo Capricorn,And that great mornWherein a God was born,Whose story none can tellBut He whose every word's a miracle.

To-day Almightiness grew weak;The Word itself was mute and could not speak.

That Jacob's star which made the sunTo dazzle if he durst look on,Now mantled o'er in Bethlehem's night,Borrowed a star to show Him light!He that begirt each zone,To whom both poles are one,Who grasped the zodiac in His handAnd made it move or stand,Is now by nature man,By stature but a span;Eternity is now grown short;A King is born without a court;The water thirsts; the fountain's dry;And life, being born, made apt to die.

Chorus.

Then let our praises emulate and vieWith His humility!Since He's exiled from skiesThat we might rise,— From low estate of menLet's sing Him up again!Each man wind up his heartTo bear a partIn that angelic choir and showHis glory high as He was low.Let's sing towards men good-will and charity,Peace upon earth, glory to God on high!Hallelujah! Hallelujah!

Jeremy Taylor.

CHRISTMAS IN CUBA.

On the hill-side droops the palm, The air is faint with flowers, In the wondrous, dream-like calmOf tropical morning hours. Like a mirror lies the bay, And softly on its breast, In the glow of coming day, The vessels sway at rest.

Through the tremulous air I hearThe chiming of Christmas bells, As the sun rises burning and clearOver the ocean swells. And birds with singing sweetProclaim the glorious mornWhen angels thronged to greetThe Christ-child newly born.

But with strong desire I sighFor a frozen land afar, Under a cold gray sky, Where glistens the northern star; Where a winter of rest and sleepEmbraces mountain and plain, And meadows their secret

Dearer the pine-clad hillsAnd valleys wrapped in snow, Dearer the ice-bound rills, And roaring winds that blow, Than this tropical calm, and perfumeOf jasmine and lily and rose, These flowers that always bloom, This nature without repose.

Alas for the delightOf a distant fireside, Where loving hearts uniteTo keep this Christmas-tide! Where the hemlock and the pineSweet memories recall, As their fragrant boughs entwineAround the panelled wall.

O Christ-child pure and fair, Draw near and dwell with me; Thy love is everywhere, On land and on the sea. I grasp Thy saving hand, And while to Thee I pray, Alone, in a foreign land, I bless this Christmas-day.

Helen S. Conant.

FAREWELL TO CHRISTMAS.

Now farewell, good Christmas,Adieu and adieu,I needs now must leave thee,And look for a new;For till thou returnest,I linger in pain,And I care not how quicklyThou comest again.

But ere thou departest,I purpose to seeWhat merry good pastimeThis day will show me;For a king of the wassailThis night we must choose,Or else the old customsWe carelessly lose.

The wassail well spicedAbout shall go round,Though it cost my good masterBest part of a pound:The maid in the butteryStands ready to fillHer nappy good liquorWith heart and good-will.

And to welcome us kindlyOur master stands by,And tells me in friendshipOne tooth is a-dry.Then let us accept itAs lovingly, friends;And so for this Twelfth-dayMy carol here ends.

New Christmas Carols, a.d. 1661.

THE NEW YEAR.

Hark, the cock crows, and yon bright starTells us the day himself's not far;And see where, breaking from the night,He gilds the western hills with light.With him old Janus doth appear,Peeping into the future year,With such a look, as seems to say,The prospect is not good that way.Thus do we rise ill sights to see,And 'gainst ourselves to prophesy;When the prophetic fear of thingsA more tormenting mischief brings,More full of soul-tormenting gall,Than direst mischiefs can befall.But stay! but stay! methinks my sight,Better inform'd by clearer light,Discerns sereneness in that brow,That all contracted seem'd but now.His reversed face may show distaste,And frown upon the ills are past;But that which this way looks is clear,And smiles upon the new-born year.

He looks, too, from a place so high,The year lies open to his eye;And all the moments open areTo the exact discoverer.Yet more and more he smiles uponThe happy revolution.Why should we then suspect or fearThe influences of a year,So smiles upon us the first morn,And speaks us good as soon as born?Plague on't! the last was ill enough,This cannot but make better proof;Or, at the worst, as we brush'd throughThe last, why so we may this too;And then the next in reason shouldBe superexcellently good:For the worst ills (we daily see)Have no more perpetuityThan the best fortunes that do fall;Which also bring us wherewithalLonger their being to supportThan those do of the other sort;And who has one good year in three, And yet repines at destiny, Appears ungrateful in the case, And merits not the good he has.

Then let us welcome the new guestWith lusty brimmers of the best; [Pg 233] Mirth always should good fortune meet, And render e'en disaster sweet; And though the princess turn her back, Let us but line ourselves with sack, We better shall by far hold outTill the next year she face about.

Charles Cotton.

A HAPPY NEW YEAR.

The old year now away is fled, The new year it is enteréd, Then let us now our sins down-tread And joyfully all appear. Let's merry be this holiday, And let us now both sport and play, Hang sorrow, let's cast care away: God send you a happy New Year!

For Christ's circumcision this day we keep, Who for our sins did often weep; His hands and feet were wounded deep, And His blessed side with a spear. His head they crownéd then with thorn, And at Him they did laugh and scorn, Who for to save our souls was born: God send us a happy New Year!

And now with New-Year's gifts each friend Unto each other they do send; God grant we may all our lives amend, And that the truth may appear. Now like the snake cast off your skin Of evil thoughts and wicked sin, And to amend this New Year begin: God send us a happy New Year!

And now let all the company In friendly manner all agree, For we are here welcome, all may see, Unto this jolly good cheer. I thank my master and my dame, The which are founders of the same; To eat, to drink now is no shame: God send us a merry New Year!

Come, lads and lasses every one, Jack, Tom, Dick, Bessy, Mary, and Joan, Let's cut the meat up unto the bone, For welcome you need not fear; And here for good liquor we shall not lack, It will whet my brains and strengthen my back; This jolly good cheer it must go to wrack: God send us a merry New Year!

171

Come, give's more liquor when I do call,I'll drink to each one in this hall;I hope that so loud I must not bawl,But unto me lend an ear;Good fortune to my master send,And to my dame which is our friend,Lord bless us all, and so I end:God send us a happy New Year!

New Christmas Carols, a.d. 1642.

NEW-YEAR'S GIFTS.

The young men and maids on New-Year's day, Their loves they will present With many a gift both fine and gay, Which gives them true content: And though the gift be great or small, Yet this is the custom still, Expressing their loves in ribbons and gloves, It being their kind good-will.

Young bachelors will not spare their coin, But thus their love is shown; Young Richard will buy a bodkin fine And give it honest Joan. There's Nancy and Sue with honest Prue, Young damsels both fair and gay, Will give to the men choice presents again For the honor of New-Year's day.

Fine ruffs, cravats of curious lace, Maids give them fine and neat; For this the young men will them embrace With tender kisses sweet: And give them many pleasant toys To deck them fine and gay, As bodkins and rings with other fine things For the honor of New-Year's day.

It being the first day of the year, To make the old amends, All those that have it will dress good cheer, Inviting all their friends To drink great James's royal health, As very well subjects may, With many healths more, which we have store, For the honor of New-Year's day.

A Cabinet of Choice Jewels, a.d. 1688.

THE END OF THE PLAY.

The play is done; the curtain drops,Slow falling to the prompter's bell;A moment yet the actor stopsAnd looks around to say farewell.It is an irksome word and task;And, when he's laughed and said his say,He shows, as he removes the mask,A face that's anything but gay.

One word ere yet the evening ends;Let's close it with a parting rhyme,And pledge a hand to all young friends,As fits the merry Christmas-time.On life's wide scene you, too, have parts,That fate erelong shall bid you play;Good-night! with honest, gentle heartsA kindly greeting go alway.

Come wealth or want, come good or ill,Let young and old accept their part,And bow before the Awful Will,And bear it with an honest heart.Who misses or who wins the prize,Go, lose or conquer as you can;But if you fail, or if you rise,Be each, pray God, a gentleman.

A gentleman, or old or young! (Bear kindly with my humble lays);The sacred chorus first was sungUpon the first of Christmas days;The shepherds heard it overhead,The joyful angels raised it then;Glory to heaven on high, it said,And peace on earth to gentle men.

My song, save this, is little worth;I lay the weary pen aside,And wish you health, and love, and mirth,As fits the solemn Christmas-tide.As fits the holy Christmas birth,Be this, good friends, our carol still—Be peace on earth, be peace on earth, To men of gentle will.

William Makepeace Thackeray.

The End

www.ingramcontent.com/pod-product-compliance
Lightning Source LLC
Chambersburg PA
CBHW070650290526
45790CB00001B/252